Truth with No Proof

Stories That Portray the Mystery of Unseen Energy

Paula Bourassa

Copyright © Written by Paula Bourassa
ISBN 13: **978-0-9993197-3-4**
Library of Congress Control Number: 2017912782
LCCN Imprint Name: Paula A Bourassa
Los Angeles, CA

This book is dedicated to anyone who has allowed their logic to overrule their inner knowing.

Contents

Mr. EB, the Talking Horse	1
Sentimental Buddy	3
Delicate Nervous System	7
Beagle People Pleaser	9
Feline Gratitude	15
Return of the Jester	17
The Bathroom Snail	21
Mother in Transport	23
Anne	25
Racing to Enrique	29
Unknown Anniversary Date	33
Ode to an Ovary	37
Attending Your Own Funeral	41
Mystery Man	45
Cottage Invitation	49
Pressure Cooker in My Head	53
Intuitive Diagnosis	57
Rock on the Gravel Pathway—Part I	59
Relocation of Pet Rock—Part II	69
My Life as a Rock—Part III	75
Super Rock—Part IV	81
The Thirty-Six-Year-Old Wart	87

Psyche Surgery	91
Shaky Knees	97
The Death of a Dead Man	99
Athena	109
Hitting the Skids	113
Cursing a Blue Streak	117
Feeling Like a Failure	121
Lady in the Hospital	127
Mary Comes Alive	131
Purple Light in the Bush	137
Tag Team Seals	143
Bouncing off the Walls	147
A Planet Named Gaia	149
Crop of Energy	153
Ascension Flight 19	161
Sara's Story	165

Preface

As a human being having a spiritual experience, I don't proclaim a right way or a wrong way to proceed. I am not an authority on anything, nor do I have proof to substantiate certain things that have happened to me other than to say that the richest moments of my life have been based on unexplained occurrences, whose existence you cannot prove. Even though life on earth demands black-and-white proof to verify or establish credibility, I live and am supported in the energy of spirit, the invisible world from which I came prior to incarnating, and the same place I'll return to one day when my earthly sojourn is complete. The eternal spark of creation endures and exists in everything. No representation of that energy is trivial or meaningless. I am living proof.

Mr. EB, the Talking Horse

Ebony was a real prince of a horse. He was also known as Eb, Ebbie, Eboush, and many other nicknames, which were easy to come up with because he was such a sociable character. He was next door to my mare Lulu's stall, which made it easy for him to keep a curious eye on us with interest in everything we were doing. Nobody paid much attention to him, and so he passed the time away being nosey.

His people were too busy to properly take care of him, so when the lady who owned the property mentioned she was looking for someone to take him over, I was quite certain he'd accept me as his new owner and be a happy addition to my family. He was full of joy, and everyone who boarded at the barn loved him for his willingness to be a great friend and companion.

I was riding him one day and had the idea to go down a pathway, when much to my delight, he turned to make the quick right before receiving the cue to do so. Or I'd be sitting on him and only have the thought to trot, and that is exactly what he'd do without being asked by a foot signal or use of the reins. He was a strong mental communicator, and it was fun to know I could receive his thoughts and he could receive mine.

But one episode stands out as the cream of the crop and shows why he was so special. One morning, I was busily grooming Lulu when I heard a loud male voice say, "Hey, could you do that for me?" Startled, since I was the only one at the barn that day, I looked up and realized it was Ebony, sticking his head out the stall-door window to watch me brush Lulu's tail and mane. He had no problem at all asking for what he wanted because he was the incredible talking horse, Mr. EB.

Sentimental Buddy

Lulu would never take a chance with mental telepathy or risk me missing her important message; she'd just show me her rump! Ebony was very good friends with Lulu because prior to me taking him over, he'd been her side-by-side stablemate for over a year and would cry at the top of his lungs if we left the stables to go out for a ride.

I could hear him as we walked away, which never was a good feeling, especially knowing he would yell and pace until we returned. Once she was within view, he would immediately settle down. I don't think he was so upset about getting off the property himself as much as he just didn't like it when she was away. They were closely bonded, and many times I would see them outside their stalls in the open paddock area intently staring at each other in silent communication.

When EB came under my care, I was fortunate to have made friends with another horse lover and fellow boarder who loved him too, and this made it possible for us all to go out together. It was never a dull moment, and even though my friend had an affinity for him, he had a mind of his own, and she found it difficult at times to get him to listen.

Even so, any frustration fell away because you always felt

his heart was in the right place. He was a seasoned veteran and had received his fill of taking orders. He'd sent me the thought on more than one occasion that carrying people on his back and having to figure out lots of mixed signals regarding which way they wanted to go and how fast had given him job burnout.

His original owner had leased him out for a time, and I think he had to deal with many novice riders pulling on the bit in his mouth or being rough with him, so he figured now was the time in the safety of true love to do things his way.

This became apparent when his rider asked him repeatedly to make a sharp left to avoid running into someone's mailbox, and he continued to belligerently plow straight ahead, taking down the mail post in his slow but powerful stride. I knew that for safety purposes, he needed to obey her commands, but somehow when I looked at the expression on his face, I could only love our friend for not being a strict taskmaster. She was never rough with him and made up for a lot of other crap he went through in his previous experiences with riders who couldn't care less.

The other time he decided to be in charge, she had asked him to move over since we were riding by parked cars and needed the extra room to pass comfortably, and when he refused, there was nothing she could do to stop him. He plodded on, sideswiping someone's rear-view mirror seemingly without a care in the world. When we turned around to see it dangling by a thread, we did our best to handle repairs and get back to the barn without further incident. This, of course, wasn't funny unless you were familiar with his personality. We tried to ignore the obvious by just accepting that our beloved Ebony was a stubborn old man. They were joyful times because EB and Lulu got to go out together.

Very sadly, the day came when Lulu broke a bone in her foot and had to be put down. The vet didn't understand how it happened, but it didn't matter. I had to rely on his medical and professional opinion on the best and most humane thing to do. It was crazy that something like this could happen just milling around in her stall. He didn't think there was an option that would really leave her feeling happy and healthy, so it was the loving thing to do. It was by far one of the most excruciating days of my life. The grief made stillness sound like noise.

I had talked to Ebony and did my best to transmit thoughts he'd understand, hoping he wouldn't suffer once he realized she was gone. He probably did know on some level, but nothing seemed to make it easier for either of us. When she didn't return to her stall after the vet's visit that day, he started clamoring at the top of his lungs. The next day, the stable hand at the ranch said he cried all night long. He was inconsolable.

I was there with him all day and some of the night, but feeling his sorrow in addition to my own had sickened me since I knew there wasn't much I could do for him. He would blink his eyelashes, and water would trickle out like he was crying. Trying to quiet my own despair at seeing him in such a state, I wished for a magic wand. I didn't know what else to do but place my hands on him, massaging his neck and back with a loving energy. Seconds later, with my whole heart in it, I realized the love that flowed from my hands was the magic wand, because there was calm, and it seemed to be enough. Love is all we got.

This story is dedicated to anyone who says animals do not have souls or feelings.

Delicate Nervous System

Filling Lulu's water bin and watching her placidly eating breakfast was always an enjoyable task, but when she started wildly swishing her tail and kicking her back left leg out to the side, a bit of worry set in. After one of these sidekicks, she would gingerly touch her toe to the ground but not put any weight on that leg, as though it hurt her to stand on it. I wondered what could be wrong and hoped it wasn't a painful spasm or hoof problem.

I was used to having smaller animals like cats and dogs you could easily put in the car for a vet trip if something went wrong, but my biggest fear of having an animal her size was that I might not be able to get help fast enough and she'd suffer. Even if it was for only a few minutes, the very thought drove me crazy, so I tried not to focus on the fact that she was favoring one side and not even attempting to stand on all four. She was acting so peculiar that I couldn't imagine what would be distressing her since she had seemed fine moments earlier while chewing on her morning alfalfa flake.

She was a high-strung mare, and you really had to know her to understand it was a major accomplishment just to approach her in a way that'd leave you in her good graces. Guesstimating on how to get close enough without causing further aggravation, I inched my way over to take a closer look. Much to my surprise, a little ladybug had flipped over on her left hip and was struggling to get right side up. Wow, what a commotion over such a tiny bug squirming on her butt, and what a relief to know it wasn't anything worse.

On her behalf, I'll have to say I witnessed this sensitivity often. Even if I spoke to her in a slightly raised voice, she'd immediately react to my tone by throwing her ears back. I thought about what a wonderful commercial she'd make for the humane treatment of all animals with such a demonstration of a delicate nervous system. She was a fine example that animals are sensitive beings and have an incredible "feeling" response not only to their environment but how we treat them.

Beagle People Pleaser

My sister and her family were planning a ten-day out-of-state vacation, hoping to hurdle over the only major issue—finding a dog sitter for their beagles, Bella and Molly. The situation required extra care because Bella needed seizure medication at exact times twice a day. The thought of hiring a student for this job or other casual acquaintance left my sister stressed on who she could trust to handle the details and not worry about a pill getting missed.

They were also used to being walked once a day, and not being well disciplined made it a challenge to handle them, manage poop bags, and return without casualty. My niece and nephew were going along on the trip, and even though they were both in their twenties and out of the house already, my sister and her husband's nest stayed full of beagle children, Bella and Molly.

The dogs went from being rescued by my sister from dire situations to becoming instantly cherished family members. Bella was rescued very young, when her owner was in the act of drawing his shotgun to put her down because she was not a good hunting dog, so he saw no further reason to keep her. A neighbor witnessed this attempt at her life and saved her from the ordeal by getting her to an organization for abused animals. She developed seizures a short time after being adopted by my sister but kept well if the medication was properly managed at twelve-hour intervals.

Molly was a couple of years older and previously owned by someone but turned out to the street, where she later got picked up and put in the pound. My niece had seen an ad for homeless animals and convinced her dad to make a trip to the shelter, where they fell in love with Molly and took her home.

Both dogs suffered from separation anxiety, which made going places a challenge since they were never left alone longer than four hours. They kept a close eye on my sister and never let her out of their sight. To have peace and sleep well at night, she let the dogs sleep in a crib next to her bed. This way, they saw she was there and would go to sleep; otherwise, it was about crying and whimpering all night long or shuffling about on the bed, meaning no sleep for my sister and her husband.

The only other problem occurred if you'd bring out a broom or fly swatter. They'd run for cover and cower. Sadly, even after ten years of having a loving family, the memory of being swatted didn't fade away. My heart went out to everyone in this matter. Coming from Scotland to handle the dog-sitting job was a huge endeavor, but I so appreciated my sister giving the dogs a home that it pleased me to be there and give them the best possible care so all could go and enjoy their vacation time.

I arrived a few days early to adjust to the house noises, buttons, gadgets, and so on. The dogs remembered me from previous visits, and it wouldn't be the first time I was their dog sitter. Even though they were very sad for a day or two when my sister left the house, they eventually resigned themselves to being cared for by their auntie, who they understood loved them very much.

It was quite the experience, but we managed, and I enjoyed their company. Each night after a walk we would settle in for a bit of TV, and then at bedtime, the procedure was hoisting each of them up into the crib, followed by the delivery of a few doggie treats for going along with the protocol. Like children, they tested me, whimpering as soon as the light went off to see if I would have mercy on their cause and let them sleep on the bed.

I knew that would make it very difficult for my sister when she returned so thought better of it and just let them be. After the second night, they got the idea that I wasn't going to give in and just lay down and went to sleep.

The time quickly approached when my sister would be

returning home, and my goal was for everyone and everything to be in great shape. I decided the night she was to return, the dogs and I would sleep in the guest bedroom, so her bedding would get washed, and they'd have freshly cleaned sheets to crawl into.

They weren't expected till 2:00 a.m., and while changing the bed linen, I was thinking how much the dogs would like the idea and be happy if they got to sleep on the bed with me in the other room. This plan was in my thoughts early in the morning, when I took the sheets off to wash, and by noon, Molly was lying on the bed in the guest room. I was astonished because the dogs never went in that room and certainly hadn't been in there the whole time their family was away.

The day progressed, and after the evening walk, it was TV time. Bella was with me, but Molly had disappeared. It was highly unusual because if one was on the couch, the other would be close by draped on the other side like a matching bookend. I got up to look for her, worried she might not be feeling well. That was the only time she'd ever leave Bella's side and crawl under the couch until she felt better, but after checking, I found she was not there.

I walked down the hallway and was surprised to see her lying on the bed again in the guest room. She had apparently received my thought via mental telepathy as to where she'd be sleeping that night and, wanting to show me she already knew what the plan was, hunkered down prior to the command to do so. Some people have been termed "people pleasers" for their accentuated efforts to make each other happy, but Molly, clearly, was a beagle people pleaser.

I kept going over the details in my mind of how it all occurred to double-check that I'd not said anything out loud, which would've been equally as amazing for them to understand verbal communication, but this was astounding since I'd only thought of it a couple of times in planning for my sister's return that night.

Bella and I joined her at bedtime, and there we all rested until the family came in during the wee hours of the morning. It was a pleasure to have been of service to these wonderful canines, and especially happy to have been a witness to the remarkable telepathic abilities of Molly.

Our animal friends know and understand so much more than we realize. They are so deserving of our love and care; their companionship and love is truly a gift from above.

Truth with No Proof

Feline Gratitude

I'd been visiting my friend's trailer park home one evening and noticed a gray cat hanging around her gate. My heart hurt to hear that someone had up and moved leaving him behind. As much as my friend wanted to give him a home, she couldn't take him because of her dogs.

The memory of how he sat very upright like a king in the passenger's seat for the ride home that night, proudly looking out the window, healed the ache, for clearly from his expressive posture, he felt very pleased he'd been invited to go home with me. He blended into our household, immediately taking delight in every event, from perching on the bathroom counter every morning to watch my husband shave to sitting in the fruit bowl in the middle of the kitchen table for a prime position to observe the daily activity. His antics were joyful, so we named him Jester.

Late one Friday afternoon, I was lying on my bed hoping the pain in my tooth would subside, but due to it being the weekend, the dentist office was closed until Monday morning, so I wasn't feeling very hopeful. The tooth had been in question for some time but decided to flare up very quickly, throbbing relentlessly with a dull ache. I wasn't there very long when Jester jumped up on the bed and laid down with half of his body on top of me. He purred affectionately and seemed to be generating a huge amount of heat, which was soothing.

He didn't stay in that position long, but five minutes later, when he jumped off the bed said, "I want to thank you for giving me a home when I needed one." What? Even though I knew I'd received that message via telepathy, it was as clear as hearing a man's voice fill the room.

I got up to see where he went and I realized my toothache had disappeared! The heartrending and poignant part of the story was that he suddenly passed away three days later. He had been determined to show his gratitude one final time. The soul knows when it nears completion in earthly life.

Return of the Jester

He was a fun-loving cat and lived up to his name by always providing humor and entertainment for his family. Thought to be seven or eight years old when I found him, plus the time spent with us would have made him approximately twelve to fifteen years old, when the sad day came we had to put him down. He had stopped eating suddenly, and even though I sensed it was his time, we agreed to the vet's recommendation for exploratory surgery because I knew there was no other way for my husband to have peace unless he knew everything humanly possible had been done to save him.

The surgery uncovered a mass in his stomach; however, Jester never made it and passed shortly after the breathing tube was removed. Indeed, his time to go. We all cried and moped around for days, missing his joyful presence in our home, but thankfully, as time passed, healing did occur for the grief within our hearts, and we felt less devastated.

About a year later, I was on my way to visit a friend in Malibu. Interestingly, my dream the night before indicated there was a black kitten en route at the Malibu Pet Store. It seemed ridiculous. The last thing on my mind was shopping for a kitten, but each time I tried to dismiss the idea, it zoomed back into my thoughts like an incessant pop-up. Blinded by my better judgment to be there at all, I found myself pulling into the shopping strip mall in front of the pet store.

The dream had seemed so real and in vivid color. After inquiring at the register, it was revealed that someone had rescued a small litter of kittens from a tree the previous Friday and brought them in for adoption the same day. Three days later, I was there making an inquiry. I was amazed when the store clerk took me to see three mixed-color kittens huddled together and a jet-black one on his own in the corner!

It was quite a confirmation of the accuracy of my dream, but I was still thinking to myself it was a crazy idea and decided to just go on my way and forget about it. I made a quick exit from the pet store hoping this coincidence would fade away while occupying myself in conversation with my friend.

Once I got to her place, we had a nice chat, and after feeling very satisfied from the lovely visit, I hoped to make it back home without making a pit stop at the pet store. Well, it just wasn't happening; there was a parking space waiting for me near the front door. It took only a moment for the clerk to get the kitten into a pet taxi, so he could ride safely and be near me in the passenger's seat for reassurance on the way home. Jester had been a male cat too and had also occupied the passenger seat when I took him home for the first time.

The curious thing was, at his first vet check-up, we observed he had a mark on his belly, which the doctor said may have been a hernia scar. But how did such a little tyke get a scar like that? Perhaps in the process of being birthed, and yet, in my heart, I knew it was a confirmation that this little black acting like a monkey kitten was our Jester returned to us.

His surgery scar was not just approximately, but precisely where the scar was located on the new kitten, indicating the incision mark that catapulted him to the spirit world the last time his soul was in a feline body. His tiny new self had been marked in the same place of the former body trauma to confirm it was the same soul. Not to mention, the very clear dream about where I could find him!

We had only known Jester as an adult cat, so it would have been hard to make an association based on personality quirks alone. The traits were varied since our little guy had a penchant for sharp bites to show his affection, which felt vicious at times, probably attributable to being born in the wild.

Nonetheless, the fun-loving, mischievous, make-you-laugh energy was the same. In this case, jet black too, but rather than calling him Monkey, we had the idea to honor his felineship by calling him Mokey instead.

Truth with No Proof

Court jester, or monkey, they were all aspects of the same being and overlying soul of one we'd known previously, and that gave a sense of warm satisfaction that defies words. That is what love does; it will come back whenever possible and is never lost. I had received the pleasure of many cat companions up to that point in my life, so the belly marking signaled which feline had chosen to reincarnate. A synchronistic reoccurrence and reassurance in knowing it was our beloved Jester coming home.

The Bathroom Snail

One morning after a heavy rainfall, a snail had come in through the bathroom window of the holiday cottage I was renting. Normally, I would immediately usher such a creature into a plastic container and take it outside, but thinking he might go back out on his own once he'd dried off, I decided to let him be. It was not an attractive sight, but on the other hand, keeping the windows closed to keep critters out would mean missing out on the gentle summer breeze.

Days passed, and the snail had not moved an inch, still attached to window pane just above the window opening. Weeks flew by, and I wondered if snails hibernated. As the time drew near for me to pack up and leave the abode that had been my home for several months, I wasn't sure if the next people who would occupy the place would take kindly to having a resident snail in the bathroom quarters and worried about leaving it to an uncertain fate.

This was ever present on my mind as I gathered my luggage and tidied up, noticing the snail had still not budged from the position where it entered eight weeks prior. The last day there, I'd gone to double-check the cleanliness of the bathroom and noticed the snail was gone! It had quietly slipped back out the window on the very day of my departure. Some may say just a coincidence, but after being there with me all that time, I know there was no mistake to its timely exit.

The snail had clearly received my thoughts and confirmed by going back out the window to the great outdoors. I was in awe. Mind to mind, heart to heart, all of nature contained living, breathing entities, and I had been a witness to its intelligence and awesome reminder that all of God's living things are indeed connected.

Mother in Transport

I was on high alert one morning after an unusually vivid and uncanny dream encounter. It involved escorting a lady to a doorway that she went through, but I did not. Turning away from the door and falling back at high speed through a tunnel is what startled me awake. Jumping up to write it down before forgetting any of the details, there was also great curiosity about who the lady was since I'd never seen her before.

A short time later, an e-mail came in from one of my dearest clients saying he was on his way up north from Los Angeles because his mother had suffered a stroke, and not having any further details on her condition, he felt very shaken. Mother and son were very close, and in one of their daily telephone calls, he'd most likely mentioned that I was a medium and had brought through evidence of survival and messages from their family on "the other side," including his dad, aunt, and a few family pets that had crossed over.

That's my best guess; however, the truth is he may not have shared anything at all. The soul connection may have been enough. I obviously had never met his mother, but after hearing that she'd been hospitalized, I knew in my heart, it was she who had come for help in getting to the other side.

Truth with No Proof

When he finally arrived at the medical center after his long trek, he was told she had passed away, making it clear to me she was the lady I'd taken to the doorway. Deeply honored for her trust, I shared the experience with him, feeling it would be a comfort knowing she'd been escorted to her destination in the hereafter realm.

Life continues, and since that day, he has received many, many signs from his mother letting him know she loves him, is OK, and still able to keep an eye on him! Dream or reality? In this case, it was both.

Anne

Even though Anne was my supervisor at work, we had become good friends. We were chatting away as we enjoyed the warm water in the Jacuzzi outside her apartment complex, when the subject came up of a large, gray-looking disc on her breast. It was hard for me to believe she hadn't already been to the doctor due to its size and color.

That day in the hot tub was a sorrowful eye-opener after seeing how long this matter had been overlooked, and I insisted she go to the doctor immediately. After much balking, she finally agreed to go but only to find out not much good news. She underwent treatment for breast cancer and, after many grueling months of side effects, achieved remission status.

Just turned forty years old and at the top of her field, she'd maintained a first-place status in banquet sales for a chain of beautifully located specialty restaurants. The corporation was in a major reorganization, and many changes had inspired her to get her own business up and running that utilized and complemented her wedding-banquet directorial skills.

Starting her own business had been very exciting until the day it was time for a one-year recheck at the doctor's office. I accompanied her on the appointed day and will never forget the motion of the doctor placing his hands under and alongside her neck to check her lymph nodes, when he said, "It's come back."

The tears ran down our cheeks like a river of sorrow washing away the previous hope for a new life. She hung in there without much complaint until she eventually was feeling so poorly found it necessary to have me take over one of her scheduled wedding parties because of nausea. Gratefully, she was so organized it was not an impossible task to step in for her. Although very nervous about doing so, it would be a relief to her that someone was assisting the bride and groom on their momentous day.

It was important for me to give the appearance of being confident and in charge, but in those melancholy moments, I felt in charge of nothing. A huge pit in my stomach seemed to rule the day with an emptiness and sad reminder that my dear friend was fading away.

Prior to learning of the breast can-cer-vive,[1] we had gone on a cruise to Puerto Rico and the Caribbean Islands for the time of our lives. It's the kind of fun you always remember because the laughter lifts you so high. This, along with her

---

[1]. Realizing every word carries an energetic vibration, I choose to take the onus off the threatening aspect of the term "cancer," and expand the consciousness by giving hope for survival and say, "Can-cer-vive."

genuine care and friendship, left me struggling to hold my head high.

I got through the day relieved the wedding arrangements had all gone well, but by the time I returned to give a full report of the day's activities, Anne's condition had deteriorated, so I didn't get a chance to share the results I'd hoped she'd be proud of. Shortly thereafter, she was hospitalized to receive hydration and whatever else they could offer.

It was a Saturday, and I was working a double shift at my new banquet job, a wedding in the morning and an anniversary party in the evening. She graciously had passed on her catering-business expertise to me, and that came in handy when I needed a job, and a local restaurateur needed a banquet director.

The hospital happened to be close by, so I used my break time in-between events to bring her a little cheer with "catering-business" stories of how the day was going. After a good visit and a few laughs, it was time to say good-bye.

Of all things, it was New Year's Eve, and walking quickly down the long corridor to the elevator, I was wishing I didn't have to face the busy evening ahead. Even though in a hurry to get back to work, it was like being in slow motion and taking forever to get there, but at the precise moment my finger was pressing the *L* button for lobby, Anne blurted out very loudly from her room at the end of the hallway, "I love you!"

The hall resounded in echo as all the nurses within earshot stopped in their tracks, assessing which room the yell had come from. The precision of her timing couldn't be disputed. Minutes later, I would have been in the elevator or headed toward the parking lot and not heard her. She had estimated my whereabouts like she'd been watching me on a CCTV camera. It filled my soul and left me crying all the way back to the restaurant.

Looking back so long ago, still blurry with emotion, the one thing that stands out in our treasured friendship is that she managed to say, "I love you" at such a critical time because those would be her last words to me. She slipped into a coma two days later and passed away. Soul knows.

Racing to Enrique

I dated a man named Enrique in my early twenties, and even though he was fifteen years older, our rapport was undeniable. We met at work, and after being together for several years, we estimated the next logical step would be to get married. I adored him and even had taken him to meet my family thousands of miles away, but the marriage thing just wasn't to be.

Being that number of years older, he'd already done the marriage and family bit and didn't seem keen to jump into that scenario again. My biological clock was ticking, and even though we'd been living together, once I realized we weren't on the same page in that respect, I decided to move out.

We lost touch for the next fifteen years, until one day the phone rang, and it was him. After filling him in on the status of my marriage (soon to be divorced), I couldn't believe he was calling at a time when my life was changing so drastically. Feeling very alone, and needing a place to live, it just so happened he had a room for me, accompanied by the comfort of his enduring friendship.

Even though our relationship never resumed in a man-woman fashion, the depth of "I got your back" sort of true comradery prevailed. The word "comfort" doesn't fully describe the feeling of security he brought to my life at a time when I needed something to grasp and hold on to. He was always there, and whenever I needed the room, whether it was for a few days, weeks, several months, or a year, a space in his condo would be available for me.

For personal reasons, the time had come when he needed to live with his elder sister in their late mother's family home, so I would no longer be able to stay with him once he relocated. This saddened Enrique, and as the time had come for such changes in his life, I would make periodic trips to visit whenever possible.

He had developed a condition that also had him visiting the doctor's office on a regular basis. He felt depressed from the symptoms and how it affected his overall independence as a human being but did his best to forge ahead. A year had passed since my last visit, but I awoke one morning with a distinct feeling to see him.

It was sheer craziness to even think of making a four-hour round-trip drive on a weekday, when there were other pressing things to take care of. Even so, it was like a magnetic pull strongly impressing me to just get in the car and go. Cursing myself most of the way there because the freeway was bumper to bumper, I kept thinking, "Why would you do this to yourself?" It was taxing, and I had to keep from getting boiling mad at myself.

After taking much longer than anticipated, I finally arrived to find Enrique was not feeling well but managed a smile to show his happiness to see me anyway. I was very touched after our time together, and I walked over to him in a very deliberate way, embraced his face in my hands, and gushed, "I love you, Enriquito!"

Normally, a hug good-bye was the gesture I most often used to express my affection for anyone, but in this case, I couldn't have slowed my roll if I tried; it poured out of me like a flooding river. His sister was happy I managed to get there when I did and didn't seem to mind it was an unannounced call because the following day they both had doctor appointments and wouldn't have been there. Feeling content with my effort, I hopped back in the car to make the long trip back home.

The shock of my life came on the following day when his sister called to say they had been at the doctor's office waiting to be seen and, after a short time, looked up from her magazine to find Enrique in a slump and barely breathing. After letting out a shriek, help came from all directions as they were in a hospital, and the staff quickly tried to resuscitate him with all sorts of equipment. He never regained consciousness though and passed on later that evening.

    I was in awe thinking about the trip I'd made the day before to see him. Even if I'd not been able to make it, I would have had to settle for simply knowing in my heart that he knew I loved him, but there was still nothing quite like the opportunity at one of life's transitional doorways to commemorate love by saying in person— "I Love You." My soul had beckoned where its highest choice was to be.

Unknown Anniversary Date

Repeatedly impressed with an urge to look over the top of my desk, specifically, a stack of papers and some pictures of my dad didn't make sense because I'd already been over there once and didn't see anything unusual. Intent on following through with a long overdue, but well-organized closet-cleaning mission, I wasn't willing to get deterred or easily sidetracked by anything.

It didn't matter what the plan was; I kept naturally gravitating over to the desktop for another glance, feeling like I might have missed something important. I finally paused, looking at a picture of me and my dad that seemed to be the center point of my attention. I collected a few moments to think of him and wondered what was going on for me to be continually drawn to the pictures.

After just speaking to him a week prior on the telephone, it wasn't like there was an unordinary urge to contact someone you'd not been in touch with for a long time. Feeling satisfied that I'd just spoken to him, not knowing what else it could be, released the nagging sensation so I could go about my duties.

The following morning, I was sitting quietly with my cup of coffee and had a distinct feeling it was someone's birthday or anniversary. I started flipping through my calendar to peruse the most recent weeks to see if I could locate a celebration or anniversary to match the strong feeling of possibly forgetting someone's special date. Couldn't find a thing, but the impression stayed with me. I just figured it would be revealed as the day proceeded, and I took my mind off focusing on it. Well, what I didn't expect was a call from my brother around noontime to say our father had passed away that morning. He had gone out to shovel the driveway, and after the first or second shovel full, down he went.

We were not sure if it was a heart attack, or something like what happened to his brother a year prior, who was also shoveling snow and suddenly passed away from an aneurysm behind his heart. My brother was called to the hospital morgue to properly identify him, and what stood out was his report that when the blanket was pulled back, dad had a smile on his face. Here I had been so impressed with whose special day it was, and come to find out it was my father's going-home day. His smile gave me the comfort to know that returning home to God's estate was a day to celebrate!

The last thing I ever imagined but couldn't argue with the fact that I kept getting it was a day of celebration, which is what ultimately helped to ease the shock and grief. The knowing, even though not knowing exactly why I kept being drawn to his picture was the only way my personality could receive the energetic broadcast of his upcoming transition, like an invisible radio wave.

There'd been another clue. I'd had a dream the night before he passed, but thinking it represented my own passing, and not wanting to startle anyone by repeating it, I kept it to myself. In the dream, a man had a little girl by the hand; she was under two years old and gliding behind him as they sped upward through a narrow tunnel. There seemed to be throngs of people on either side of the passageway, and they were making a lot of noise as they reached out to us passing by. We came to a doorway, and as the man walked on through, he let go of the girl's hand, and she tumbled backward at an incredible speed.

This sensory experience quickly awakened me with an uncertainty of what it all meant. Then, the day unfolded when I received word my father had suddenly departed earth, leading me to believe the man in my dream was my dad, and the little girl must have been me. I don't know if it was his soul's knowing connecting to me, or my own soul knowing of his imminent transition that manifested as a dream—interpretation didn't matter at that point; he was home.

Truth with No Proof

Ode to an Ovary

It was the beginning of the weekend, and I was looking forward to enjoying time with my best friend and her husband. Late Friday afternoon, there was a sharp pain in my abdomen that continued sporadically throughout the night. It was noticeable enough to mention the last time I felt anything similar was during ovulation in my younger years.

At my age, to feel this specific pain on my lower right side was surreal, and the throb flooded me with much memory. It was long ago, my husband and I had been trying to start a family by paying close attention to monthly ovulation cycles to ensure success. After five years of trying, it's not something you forget so easily when month after month showed no sign of a pregnancy.

Even though my husband wasn't sure if he could have children due to a medication his mother took while pregnant with him, the tests were not 100 percent conclusive, so we hoped for a miracle. The doctor had verified that everything seemed to be in proper working order for me, but long story short, no such luck. We ended up adopting children from a foreign country, which brought to the table many unforeseen problems. This put a strain on our relationship, and our marriage eventually ended in divorce.

Saturday morning when my friends asked about the pain, I reported that due to its sharp persistence and pulsing on and off throughout the night, I wondered if something else might be wrong. Thankfully, late that evening it started to subside, and by midday Sunday, the pain had cleared.

The most remarkable thing was to receive word Monday morning that my ex-husband had passed away suddenly Sunday evening around 7:00 p.m. The shock was one thing, but then later connecting the dots related to the ovary pain was extremely poignant. During my marriage to Marius, my body had sacredly prepared for a pregnancy by preserving an egg or two hoping for a conception. Two days prior to his passing, my soul knew he was about to leave the earth plane, and my body began the process to release the ovum knowing I would no longer need them!

The timing was pristine. The ovulation cycle completed itself around noontime on Sunday, and Marius transitioned into the spirit world hours later that same day. The supreme sensitivity and astuteness of my physical body, in union with mind, and spirit, regarding my ex-husband left me gobsmacked. How my soul knew that Marius would pass by letting go of the dream we had shared by releasing the last remnant of physical energy that wove us together was incredible to me. A sure case of how our own soul light weaves out to those we connect with. Having my friends as witnesses certainly made the event feel even more credible and profound.

Truth with No Proof

Attending Your Own Funeral

My soul was delighted Marius didn't have to feel the heaviness of this earth plane any longer, but rest of me still felt somewhat sickened with grief. Even though divorced, the love between us remained. Often, we would talk on the phone just to commiserate or make each other feel better about the ongoing conundrum with our adopted daughters, which never seemed to improve but only worsened. As much as we put our best efforts forward, all that remained was heartache, so it didn't surprise me he had passed suddenly from heart trouble.

The image was of him standing with his hand on his hip looking at me with a cheesy smile and beaming with pride. I'd seen his face for hours in my clairvoyant vision and thought maybe it was a photograph someone put up for his memorial service that day, but after checking with his family, there was no such picture. I was more accustomed to seeing and identifying spirit for others, so it didn't register at first that he was coming directly to see me.

He transmitted a message that he was proud of me as a lightworker and could understand it now that he was dwelling in the finer etheric realms. What a great message to receive because there were many times in our marriage he felt perplexed by such matters. He also indicated by his happy expression that he'd been blessed with the beauty of unconditional love upon his transition and was at ease from acquiring a new understanding of the real meaning of love.

During this communication, I was aware of three beings standing in the corner of the room. These were the guides who assisted him in returning to earth to say "hello" and attend his own funeral. He was curious what people would say about him, and thankfully, many praises were given from the many employees he'd helped over the years, which added to his joy. Then, at the end of the day, it was those same three guides who were there again to assist in taking him back to the other side.

They wanted to ensure his round-trip excursion was successful, and so they led him back through the same portal opened for his entry since that was the gentlest way. Being so newly transitioned required some help in the early lessons of visiting earth until you acquire the skills to come and go on your own.

It gave me comfort like no other to see him happy and content. He was free from the chains that bound him on earth and was pleased to move on. After this uplifting vision, grief didn't seem to be an appropriate emotion, although the sadness of him not being here anymore lingered. Spiritual awareness dismissed the sorrow; however, I've also accepted that part of being human is that we do miss someone we've loved when he or she is no longer here.

Truth with No Proof

Mystery Man

Standing in a check-in line at the airport, I couldn't help but notice the guy in front of me. He would occasionally turn around and look at me over the top of his dark sunglasses in a flirtatious way. I couldn't imagine anyone admiring me at that hour in the morning with toothpicks holding my eyes open. It was beyond comprehension but grabbed my curiosity. He was in the middle of checking in his guitar case and luggage and at the same time turning around frequently to look at me. He seemed too young, although, his age may have been disguised by his youthful stance and traveling minstrel demeanor.

I scanned myself, plain faced and barely awake, and couldn't imagine looking attractive. Even after this critique from my personality, I was feeling flattered by the noticeable amount of attention, and my next thought was, "Well, I don't look that bad either." Once he finished at the counter, I stepped up and managed my own details and, with boarding pass in hand, headed toward the departure gate.

Trying to stay focused on the directions for getting to the proper terminal, I breezed down a long corridor looking for the next signpost realizing I was still very preoccupied with the earlier energetic exchange. This *Twilight Zone* plot thickened when the same man from check-in approached me from the opposite direction, asking if I knew which way he needed to go. He was very sweet, and there was a tenderness in his voice but not in a hurry or the anxious rush of someone who was really lost.

Now, I was thinking to myself how strange it was and at the same time suggested we go to the information desk right around the corner. So, there we stood in side-by-side lines, one for domestic, and one for international. I was trying hard not to stare too intently because he really reminded me of someone, but I couldn't put my finger on it. Long dark hair, slender, dark shades, dark eyes, guitar case? Hmmm. After speaking briefly to the agent, he confidently went off in a different direction, and we smiled at each other, as I affectionately gestured with a wave and the words, "Hope you have a good trip."

I got to the waiting lounge realizing I had some time before my gate would be announced and collected myself to relax. Moments later, I started to cry uncontrollably and ran to the nearest toilet to hide behind a closed door so as not to draw further attention to myself. I couldn't stop. The middle of a busy airport is the last place you expect the floodgates of grief to open. I'd been so distracted by airport tasks that it didn't register that the man flirting with me had been an exact double for my friend Greg, whom I'd been crazy about.

I'd always had the hots for him. He and I had an infinity for each other, which, at best, culminated one day in a wonderful "make-out" session on the couch. The passion blinded me, so I never understood why it didn't evolve into the progression of a full love, but it wasn't meant to be.

I couldn't see at the time that the person I was in a primary relationship with would have been hurt from that scenario, and so the blossoming energy was kept at bay. I figured this must be why God gave us an imagination; it was a way to make believe and dream about how it might have been.

I had met him and his mother early on in my spiritual journey, and it was a gift to have found like-minded friends with similar sensitivity. They were both very special to me for that reason and because many Sunday afternoons they spent sitting with me as a platform for the development of my mediumship as a channel for spirit. So, there was a spiritual bond between all of us that was sacred.

Years passed and when I heard he'd gotten married, I was pleased he'd found someone, and at the same time, I was thinking, "Why couldn't it have been me?" There was a depth of feeling for him that was indescribable and impossible to find words that would express or convey such feeling, so not knowing what to do with it, I put it on a shelf.

Then, a short time later, after hearing he had passed away suddenly in his sleep, there was even more emotion to stockpile. I knew he had some medical issues but mostly aware that he was just done here on earth, I did my best to accept it, rationalize it, attempt to make sense of it, and then add it to the tub of tears already on the shelf.

But now, in the middle of a very busy airport, I couldn't find a shelf anyplace! The realization of my best efforts to put all that feeling aside for so long couldn't be held any longer, and it gushed. The mystery man matched the description of Greg to a *T*, and he had left quite an impression on me.

I wasn't aware so much grief was still within me, and had it not been for the brief encounter, it all would have stayed buried. I know there is no sense of time on the other side, but even though he'd only been over there less than two years, I found it remarkable and reassuring that he'd used his spiritual abilities to manifest back in 3-D reality that way. The mock-up was a near double of himself!

I was touched that he thought of me and, even in his new life on the other side, although separated by distance, space, and time, still found a way to acknowledge love is never lost, and love never dies.

Cottage Invitation

The hiking trails and beautiful scenery were boundless in Scotland, and locating an affordable one-bedroom flat was thanks to the friends who owned it. Over the years, I had also met a man from a different village in a similar bucolic setting and decided to pay him a visit. He had a granny flat to let, and it turns out the day I visited, his lodger gave the notice to depart.

I'd stayed there off and on over the years, but my last stay got cut short due to a mix-up in communication signals. Hearing the news of his tenant's intention to vacate sparked a feeling of interest since that would make it available to me. My wish to blend the heart and soul of me was urging to be near this long-lost friend. Looking forward to revisiting the area was great, and the comfort of my friend's companionship was wonderful, but the crux of the decision on where to be was that I also felt at home where I was.

Even though the great synchronicity of the tenant giving his notice on the day I was there for a visit was showing me it was in flow, I felt a bit apprehensive as you always do when making a big change and hoped for some extra confirmation or sign that it was in harmony for me to be there. I had been in a regularly sized apartment and would be going to a single small room, which was a lot to imagine since my cosmetic case seemed to fill the entire bathroom on its own.

After some deliberation, making the decision to relocate was in motion, and the morning I was to make my way up north, I was quietly doing my yoga stretches, when a very peculiar smell waft across the room. It was distinctively sharp and pungent, like nothing I'd ever smelled before, so I knew it must have an equally definitive meaning.

Later that day, when I arrived in my little cubbyhole in the forest, it wasn't long before I had the clarity. The first thing my friend had to teach me was how to start a fire since my primary heat source would be a small pot-belly stove. Step one of this process included a match and a small square of a white Styrofoam material called fire-lighter. It was made of an unusual texture, smelled like detergent-strength medicine, and per instructions, a small square of it was to be placed on a mound of kindle wood and fired up, creating red hot cinders to ignite larger pieces of wood for a two-to-four-hour burn.

The practice session made the mystery clear. It was the fire-lighter! How sweet and inviting for the home spirit of that little cottage traveling to meet and greet me prior to my actual arrival with the smell of something that would be near and dear to me for staying warm in the winter. I couldn't have asked for a better confirmation to feel confident that I was in the right place at the right time. Even though it wouldn't be valued as concrete evidence to most folk, making the subtle smell connection was a prayer answered.

Truth with No Proof

Pressure Cooker in My Head

On occasion, I seemed to know where to find lost objects for people by receiving a picture in my mind of where the missing item was located. Aware throughout my life that I had some sort of something, just thought it was a combination of lucky guesswork or even something I possibly ate that triggered such knowing.

The involvement opened further by learning through a psychic reading that I could develop my sixth sense, intuition, and premonitions for full use if pursued. "Yeah right, she says that to everyone," I thought. However, the combination of my own curiosity, and the desire to investigate inspired me to read as much as I could about others who had similar abilities and what their personal experiences entailed.

Delving in taught me that the number-one tool used for increasing awareness and ability was the practice of meditation. Starting for five minutes a day seemed like a lot of time to be quiet, but with focus and determination, I gradually worked up to ten minutes.

The first five minutes was filled with mind chatter about things needing to be done that day like who was taking the trash out, leaving the remaining five minutes of stillness.

Truth with No Proof

The practice progressed into a daily session at 5:00 a.m., still leaving enough time to get ready for work and begin my day. There were many mornings I dreaded getting out from under the warm covers but stuck with it for a year until I was sitting daily for an hour from 5:00 a.m. to 6:00 a.m. in the quietude. It was a great accomplishment.

Meditating early one morning as usual toward the end of that first year, I felt a pressure sensation about to explode in the front of my head. The area in the middle of my forehead was buzzing, and the vibration of building pressure was producing an actual noise that alarmed me. It was the sound of a small earthquake if I had to do my best to identify it.

From all I'd read, it could've been some spiritual event happening in my head, but that didn't make it any less scary. It was just one of those things you don't forget, and sometime later, the understanding surfaced that my third eye (energy center in the middle of the forehead) had fully opened. This brow chakra vortex opened like a lotus blossom in full bloom, and as the petals unfolded, the vibration of the motion created sound.

The ability to locate people's lost objects well expanded into many other areas, like having visions that would come to fruition, seeing people's loved ones and pets who had passed over, seeing medical problems in people's bodies, and receiving predictions of things ahead.

It had facilitated greatly to have read stories of how other sensitives with clairvoyant, clairaudient, or clairsentient[2] abilities came to understand each of their unique spiritual gifts and was very confirming to have attended workshops geared toward this purpose, or be in classes and lectures with like-minded people. But, singlehandedly, the most important tool in my expansion was meditation.[3]

Plus, what a great calm and centered way to start the day!

---

2. Clairvoyance—clear intuitive seeing, visions, dreams, precognition; clairaudient—clear intuitive hearing noises, words, and messages not founded in third dimension; clairsentience—clear intuitive feeling as in sixth sense or having a gut feeling
3. "Days of peace and meditation will lead to your spiritual abilities opening, and you may have moments of acute knowing, synchronicities, and unusual psychic occurrences. This is a direct result of spiritual practice that triggers and activates your God/Goddess higher self, so no need to attribute these happenings to some other outside stimuli." From Paula, *Inspired by Lord Buddha, One Defining Moment* (Amazon Kindle, 2015).

Truth with No Proof

Intuitive Diagnosis

Even thinking about my sister would give me a tight feeling in the upper neck and chest area. The sensation would be magnified if I spoke to her on the phone or saw her in person. After a time, it became clear to me that the tightness worsened after communicating with her, and I realized something might be wrong physically.

After a bit of hem-hawing, and saying it was probably my imagination, she agreed to make a doctor's appointment, which I'd happily accompanied her on. The day arrived, and after the doctor checked her blood pressure, he promptly noted it was quite high and thanked me for bringing her in. Once she started taking the blood-pressure medication, I no longer experienced the gripping symptoms of tightness after thinking about her, seeing an e-mail with her name on it, or speaking to her.

The same scenario occurred regarding my ex-husband. After being with him on the phone, I'd feel very tight in the upper chest and had difficulty swallowing. This went on for at least nine months, and no amount of coaxing on my part led him to heed my advice on getting a checkup. Many more weeks passed, and one day at a scheduled doctor's visit, the doctor found out he needed a major eight bypass open-heart surgery.

Truth with No Proof

The feelings of chest distress became nonexistent for me once his heart blockage had been rectified.

Rock on the Gravel Pathway—Part I
(Rock tells his story)

I looked around one day, and the view was futile. No one was moving. They were all listless. You know if you're there long enough, you're bound to see some action, but where did all the life go? I was used to monitoring the ebb and flow of the forest by witnessing how energy presented each day on the breeze.

Lately, the soft winds were hollow, which left me feeling useless. Like a mother who invested all her time and energy in her child's rearing, once that child leaves home it was a feeling of "now what to do with my life." It was similar for me as my life-force energy felt dull with lack of application.

Eons ago, I broke free from my central parent rock during the great crush of the Ice Age. We were a family of very large boulders, and some of our neighbors were forced into each other's pathways as the earth moved through seismic and volcanic activity. I remember the day I chipped off from my foundation and left on my own to create anew. I found myself rolling at a fast speed to the valley below and finally slowed to a resting place of comfort under a very large, oak tree surrounded by sleeves of acorn shells. I practiced watching how Great Oak moved and keenly kept track of all her visitors.

They flew, crawled, and climbed. She teamed with life, and I was proud to be a part of the activity. I had found myself a new family and was embraced as one of her own, and because my shell was harder and tougher than that of her wee acorns, she soon came to notice that I had an incredible ability to withstand all sorts of weather and atmospheric conditions. I let her know that I came from the Great Rock, and my parent had taught me well, plus, I was chiseled out of core earth energy, so I fully understood the expression, "stand firm like a rock."

She and I became a great haven for many in those years, and I remained loyal to her until the day she fell to fire. Not being from the Great Rock, she was combustible, and thusly, we lost her. I did not burn due to my composition but lingered in her ashen remains. It's why my face was so dark in places. My dearest friend was gone. I knew she would always be a part of my energy family, but still missed looking up each day at her mighty presence sheltering me from sun and rain. Now, only me and other rocks remained.

There formed a need for a new family, and this time a vote was taken by members of the ground and sky on who might head up this new group. Based on my ability to hold steadfast energetically amid all sorts of environmental circumstances, I was chosen for the job of forest patron. I had managed to retain the fullness of my energy, and this had gotten everyone's attention. I felt rather bleak in those days after our group had been so compromised by the fire, but in the aftermath, I held everyone in the spirit of togetherness, and we bonded new relationships even though we were very different.

Before long, rain fell. We all soaked in the cleansing and soon afterward noticed green shoots here, there, and everywhere! Some of the beautiful souls we had previously known seemed to reincarnate before our very eyes, as tree, after tree, after tree sprung forth. A selection of many varieties appeared, some pine, some ash, and some oak. Our new family was diversified, but because they came forth out of the love in which we were all originally created to be, they were even more special to us.

Many thoughts poured through my chips and cracks, and I was proud to be a founder of much growth. I remembered my own shaky beginnings when I was forced into a different life by a great pressure tumble, and how I not only survived but became enriched with unique experiences. I held hope and strength for each member of our new little forest. The love nurtured more growth, and one day as I went to do my check

Truth with No Proof

on the flow of energy in the greenery and air, I was near shaken up as I reflected on how huge we'd become. Now, I had not just one huge tree as an umbrella over me, but many! Nestled in the pine needles was I, and very contented to *be*.

Time marched on, and as mankind grew in numbers, there were discussions on the many, diversified species in the forest and man's need to classify each one. This bred partiality for some, but not for others. What followed was the cutting down of many, creating an unforgettable sadness for those of us who called ourselves a family, no matter our size, shape, color, or smell. I did my best to keep everyone's spirit up by reminding them of how the forest could rejuvenate, as in the weeks after the fire, and that nothing could ever take away the natural force of nature as a part of our heritage on Gaia.

We loved the terra firma she provided us and were so thankful; we believe she just kept renewing herself not to sadden us further. Even so, the immeasurable unity of forest life was dwindling as we watched some of our members chopped down and disappear before we had a chance to speak to each other about what was occurring.

It left gaps of darkness where previously there had been light—until the day I looked around and saw absolutely nothing. All my colleagues had disappeared, and the tremendous enclave of raw earth energy flowing and growing in the forest had retreated. I had to remember what I had been taught about energy never being lost and in this case simply relocated.

My friends could no longer bear the disbursement and made decisions to go elsewhere. That information remains unknown to me, but what I do know is that spirit is in everything and that light can jump in and out, not like human beings who must wait to die before they can make a transition and change form.

We had that advantage in the forest; we could just go if devastation came upon us. Maybe some went to other forest locations, maybe some found a stream or body of water to flow in, and possibly some flushed into the air to be free to fly, rather than root someplace. It didn't matter, as I found myself looking around realizing there was no life where we had once created life to be. As they say in human circles, I certainly didn't want to abandon ship, like a captain who walks away in the face of pending doom before his mates.

I could feel my loyalty filling me and could not leave. I stayed the rock I'd always been. Even though my energies were no longer needed, they swelled within me, and I calculated them as devotion, because what else would they be once I felt the true essence of me.

Truth with No Proof

The growth and life of my friends had meant everything, and so that special feeling is what remained. With no place to direct my love, I stayed put. High winds had toppled many and some just left due to the stressful conditions human beings had brought to our neck of the woods. Man had come in to clean up the toppled ones with the purpose of creating a pathway for others to walk upon as one of the highlights in the local village.

It took them several years, but after being kicked about here and there, I rolled onto this gravel pathway and was left alone once the last of the trees blocking the entrance to the forest had been cleared. It was also important for men to have a driveway in and out of the woods for their own purposes to maintain control. Keep tabs on what a conifer is, and what is not, sort of thing.

Only cut branches and dried-out tree trunks I could see from my stony plate. The green tree tops off in the distance didn't really feel like trees though because as they swayed in the wind, I felt no soul there, only the remnant shell of one that once was. I kept myself occupied by trying to recall all the stories of the ancient ones and allowed them to impress me since I know no love is ever lost.

They had encouraged me to move on too and indicated I should find a new perch or family to be with that was once again teaming with life to have as joy on the earth. Somehow, I was not able to consider this suggestion. I felt maybe new life would come again to the area I had reigned over for so long, even though it wasn't happening up till this point in time. So, there I lay, half-etched into a moist pocket of ground, half exposed to whatever came my way or walked over me. I couldn't desert the place that had been my home, no matter what, even if I was the only living thing around for miles.

I was sentimental about my days with Great Oak and how we made a paradise for ourselves and those who came near, and really couldn't imagine my life-force energy being anywhere else. The ancients honor free will and would check in on me from time to time, but no one ever insisted I go.

And so, gloomy as it was, there I remained until one day I felt vibration come toward me, and a human being bent down to look at me. She touched me and then gave me a little wiggle to see if I was well established. After watching me wobble back and forth, and thinking about me, she decided to go ahead and pick me up. Ah, the warmth of her hand, I'd become as cold as my early ice-age days and was frigid. She coddled me around and was taking note of all my ridges, cracks, and grooves, turning me up, down, around, and sideways, to observe I was a rock with many faces.

Truth with No Proof

She imagined I must have a story to tell. She was a soul walker lucky for me and knew how to honor, so she asked me, "Do you want to come with me? Or stay here. Or, would you like me to take you someplace you'd enjoy more? Or stay here. OK, I guess I'll take you and trust if you're not happy you'll let me know where you'd like to be." This woman was respectful, and I puffed up even bigger with my pride and loyalty for she could feel me, and that really made my day. She felt that I had deep meaning, and that was greatly appreciated by me based on my recent experiences with humanity.

I let her know I didn't mind being a pet rock for the time being, and so off I went in her pocket. She was astonished and wondered how a magnificent being like myself could manage such a mundane task as a pet rock. But because she shared her love with me, I felt I could do anything.

It had been raining and her clothes were soaked, so she went immediately to the bath when we got home placing me in the bathroom sink. I had much practice sending thoughts to my family in the forest, and so it was easy for me to telepathically remind her she had mentioned putting me in the tub too. I understood she forgot in the hurry to get warmed up and put me in the sink instead. I fancied the idea and was glad when my thought was received. I was delighted for I'd not had that experience before, and even more pleased when she used her special gentle facial soap to give me a rub and sweet little scrub.

My first night indoors was spent on her nightstand, where I offered to share a small portion of my story. She even got up to write some of the things down not to forget—and here we are. This lady spends a lot of time alone and often thought fondly of how much she'd enjoy the company of a pet, but without a home to call her own that was not an option. So, I've stepped in. I do hope she will accept my offer of being a pet rock, so we can enjoy each other's company because her family has disbanded too.

Just because I'm a rock doesn't mean that I don't have much to share. I was rich again, for the same human hands that cut down my friends and family, now picked me up, rescued me, and gave me a new life that I hadn't been able to claim on my own. My renewed hope after meeting my human-friend is that more folk will realize there are many forms of life to appreciate on planet Earth. I am ancient, I am worthwhile, I am Earth, and I still have so much to give.

Keeper of the Forest

Truth with No Proof

Relocation of Pet Rock—Part II

I was in awe, and felt nervous at the same time, not knowing what the proper care would be for a poignant pet rock. He seemed like such a powerful being even though small sized, 2" × 2" at the most. This brought the term "feeling responsible for" to new heights. I worried about my accommodations being sufficient, and if he'd get enough sunshine and light being in the flat all day. He was a rock and used to being outside.

I'd sat him on the kitchen window sill, but he emitted such a depth of feeling, I felt uncomfortable going in the other room for too long aware of his presence just sitting there. I was certain it would cheer him up to see life-force energy in the forest again, so it was a good time to go for a walk.

If he'd been a dog, I could've just put him on a leash, so it wasn't easy trying to figure out how to position him for carrying, but after moving him around several times, from front pocket to back pocket, to side pocket, finally decided to keep him in the palm of my hand so he could see and face outward. Right, I know I'm sounding like a nut case, but his essence was so profound unless you felt it, you couldn't understand the ramifications of such a thing.

I was in a quandary just knowing what to call him: Your

Lordship, Mr. Rock, Earthman, Pet Rock, Keeper of the Forest, or nothing at all. Clutching him in my left hand would be the position, and that would have to do. As we strolled along, my mind was whirling with curiosity about what it was like to be a rock. For the longest time, I had asked God to have a greater understanding of all the kingdoms that comprise earth.

It was like having a child and hoping he'd be entertained as we walked along taking in the sights. He'd come from such an abysmal place. After finding him on the gravel pathway, it was in my heart for him to feel much happier in his new home with me, but the more I thought about how to make that happen, the more overwhelmed I became.

The responsibility felt immense, and it was impinging on my freedom. As per my understanding that is. Also, even though a wee stone, he seemed too big for me, like I'd been assigned the task of giving a revered lama a place to live. You feel intimidated because you don't know what such a noble man would be accustomed to in his daily regime.

As I looked around, the area was teeming with energy and felt pleased we had gone on that pathway. He had taken so much pride in being the keeper of the forest, and as I scanned the evergreens and pines, I couldn't help but think he'd enjoy being among them again. My primary concern was how he'd be happiest, especially after hearing his story. After reaching the top of a hill with lush greenery everywhere, I noticed a wooden gatepost and placed him atop it for a moment. I thought, "Oh God, what if I get distracted and forget I put him there and just walk away." And believe me, it was only a moment and the panic set in, like leaving your purse behind in the dressing room after trying on clothes. That was the intensity of it.

Pacing, but also aware of holding my mind very still to feel the situation, I asked Rock if he'd be happy there in the forest. I didn't hear a reply if there was one, but instead, my attention was drawn to the ground where three beautiful fresh white feathers lay. Associating them with the Native American tradition of a "giveaway" seemed to be the sign I was looking for as a signal of confirmation for him to be on top of the wood post.

Heading toward home, the experience was much to ponder, as I convinced myself leaving him in the woods was the right thing to do. But when I got home, his essence was everywhere, like he was still there. And if I'd go anywhere, it was only to feel very alone and missing him when I came back, like after relationship breaks. I had very quickly developed an attachment to this rock! I stressed over the decision and was awake most of the night worried a bird might land on his head, hoping it wouldn't expose him to distasteful ecological conditions. I didn't care for the idea of him being some ordinary perch for a creature to alight upon for the view.

I was used to the peaceful feeling that followed taking an action that was in complete harmony, and once executed, you never think of it again. But this was pulling on me, drawing me back to repeat my steps with no understanding as to why. Just after dosing off, I was startled awake with a clear vision of him in my mind's eye. I shot up and thought out loud, "Oh no! He must be coming to me because he wants to come home." I was used to seeing faces of humans and animals in my vision, but not rocks.

Sleep was out of the question. I got up, quickly got dressed, and headed out, because rest would be impossible until he was back in my hand. I walked quickly worrying about the state I might find him in. Oddly enough, I also thought about giving him another bath, like the first tub washing administered after picking him up from the gravel pathway. Only this time, it was about collecting and washing him in one of the clear flowing streams of pure water from the hills above.

I made it in under an hour, and as I approached the area anxiously strained my eyes to see if he'd been knocked off, or something else might have happened to him. "Oh my God, there he was." Still atop the post, but his head covered in bird dung. I was shocked mostly by the fact that I'd already perceived the bird, just not that it would be bird poop; hence, me having the feeling he'd need a wash. And that is exactly what happened. Back down the pathway, looking for the most beautiful babbling brook I could find, immersed him in the waters like a baptismal procedure. Ah, amid the green shrubs, plants, and trees, I felt an unseen lavishing of the Green Goddess in motion. The water was so pure and clear, and such a release of angst to have him in my hand again.

Once we arrived at the flat, back to bed I went with him once again on my nightstand. I fell back out for a couple of hours until hearing, "I'm standing, my heart out." Like here is my rock body, but the essence of me, the heart of me, has fled. Thinking I'd moved him inappropriately, my mind raced for answers or a perspective that might alleviate my feeling of wrong doing and sadness. Not to mention, the bird dung draped over one of his multifaced sides that I worried was the reason he felt forced out of his shell.

Even though probably amiss to apply my human emotion and understanding of what was right or wrong regarding the thoughts I'd received from my new friend, it haunted me to think the situation had created unhappiness for him. The very idea that I had moved Rock to an undesirable location that caused him to vacate his rock body was more than I could bear.

My Life as a Rock—Part III
(Dissertation given by Rock at morning coffee)

I've been so hurt at times. I understand what it is to have feelings. I know well the great vulnerability that is part of this existence, and how it only takes moments to destroy a heart full. And then tears spill with no place to go when left alone. It must express until empty, and then and only then, does it stand a chance of revival, like the hope and the everlasting possibilities for growth as shown to us in spring time, when seemingly deadened branches suddenly appear laden with new growth. Love is not lost, whether cut down, ravaged by fire, or taken away through any destructive force of nature. Emptied, but not lost.

Only a little splash of rain is enough to revive the life-force once visible to the human eye, and in no time blossoms are sure to follow. The cyclic events of nature provide us with the hope of renewal no matter what the reason for bare remains. Life-force energy will exude once again, as it only awaits the proper conditions to do so. In a human way, you have control over your own environment, and so that is somewhat up to the situation you create to be in. For those of us who rely on Mother for all things, a quiet waiting distresses us not, because in a matter of speaking it is instinctual, and we know we are part of a greater plan, so that is our sense of security.

A bare tree weeps, not for what was, but wears bareness just as proudly as if covered with greenery. As you understand that is the situation with many forms of plant life, your inquiring mind may wish to know if it is the same for the rocks, stones, quartz, and quarry life. It is reasonable to ask since we don't have the cover of greenery or blossoms to demonstrate our transitions. What we have is soul life.

Our soul light is a part of the Grand Mother, all for the one and one for the all, and our blossoming is that which was given to us at the beginning of time—we received her light, we were imbued with a flicker of her life-force energy, and we were set in motion to be part of the whole. We represent this splendor of life in varied diversities. Why does one of us sparkle, and another one shows nothing? Well, the best way to explain would be to say, for the same reason walking down a country pathway you see green ferns and plants, but also notice browned or dried out versions of the same. Even in the height of summertime, not all will remain green, some will be in their own changeovers outside of the spring-summer cycle.

I can only continue emptying myself to bring more. Empty allows me to always be a vessel to harbor new form. Ready, willing, and able am I to reflect Mother's abundance in all ways, trusting that as a part of her original life-streaming light, I am always sheltered and always taken care of simply because of my natural participation in her beauty and love. I am a part of it eternally, but for now in the earthly representations.

The mineral kingdom holds as much merit as any other. The plant and animal jurisdictions are maintained by the same life-force energy, they also can never really be destroyed as much as coming to their own completions and having new opportunities available to them. The keyword is "new opportunities." They never cease to exist, like the holly. We are all shapeshifting and changing every moment in time.

Humanity is playing out their parts, their roles, their dramas, and traumas as human beings. This is what they do. Kudos to the ones who know they can never be cut down, but are a part of the great cycle of Mother in the grand scheme of things, and that new life always is available to them here, there, and everywhere.

Whether renewed in any given moment due to physiological changes within the being, or reincarnated into another life after the process called death, or reestablished into another existence elsewhere in the cosmos, there is always a new way for life-force energy to be and exist.

Truth with No Proof

As a part of the mineral realm, perhaps a bit different. My graduations exist, and so do my choices for being, and up till this point in time have stayed in rock form. I have moved in and out of my shell, but for the long haul not given up the "chip off the old block" as created to be from early moments in earth's history. Chipped off, not lost. Where I roll has been where I roll. Who moves me may move me, but can never ultimately change who and what I am. My essence, my own ability to shapeshift is inherent in the spark of the flame I am.

My primary choice to keep moving in and out of the same form has been due to a sense of loyalty for my original status and place when given light by Mother. Call me old fashioned in that way, but it is out of honor for all her nature I've maintained my same form from the beginning of time. There has been no waste of time, there have only been changes to my surfaces. Some I have been in house for, inside my rock body, and some have been etched upon me when I was close by in surrounding atmospheric influences.

All my faces reflect nature and her various shifts. Shifting it is and will continue until Gaia folds in all her petals and pedestals and springs forth no more. Until her poles bend inward toward each other, and in the greeting, gather all of history, pulling in longitudes and latitudes to become one line on the graph of time. She then can ascend from round to flat. That would be her version of flatline. Be that as it may, the incredible continuation of time and life go on. Another planet-forming is of the same magnitude as another rock chipping off the block or the wall. It is of equal value in the Creator's eyes.

Where do you go when not at home in your rock, you might ask? Well, I can unite with any of Mother's lights. I can merge with molecular structures of air if I choose, or the components of fire if I wish, or swim in the moving porticos of flowing water, or just be still within the stagnant cells of a pond. I can move into what I wish. I am an incredible shrinking man if need be, or the incredible hulk. Ever shrinking or expanding as the form warrants.

All of life works this way, and why you can perceive so much ebb and flow of energy when outdoors, but not really have the words to describe it? Mostly, because much of this activity defies human description based on what has already been given by your scholars and scientists regarding existence or anyone else you give the authority to say what is accurate, true, and real. It does exist, and you identify it as comfort when being on a nature walk. It comes into your awareness, many unseen life forms that be, and breath, and even though much of its beingness is not capable of 3-D expression in a way that gives proof, you still know what you know.

And the only place to really feel this is in nature, as all the elemental kingdoms align, they do exist, not very obtusely, but they do exist, and coexist I might add with a feeling of unity that brings great joy, for it is governed by nothing but the majesty of Mother-Father-God's life-force sparking out into creation! Tick tock, tick tock, like a clock, ever steadfast, ever in motion. Everlasting.

Earthman the Rock

Super Rock—Part IV

Rock's description of life had been so full, I decided that going for a walk would be the best way to assimilate and process all that had been given. So, off we went, putting him in my pocket without worry of which way he faced. Before receiving his dissertation on life, I had worried about his view getting blocked.

He had so many uniquely etched expressions it was a challenge to know the best way to position him in my hand. His words from earlier that morning gave me the confidence to feel at ease about putting him in a pocket, my backpack, or even leaving him at home. He'd shown me that with his ability to be free, he could find his own way to be with me if that was his choice.

It was a climb up a craggy, wooded area, and my goal was to take some pictures of trees to enter in an amateur photo contest. So, with Mr. Rock in one back pocket, and my camera in the other, I was ready to go. It was amazing to see the beauty of the cut trees and how if they lie there long enough, greenery sprouts every which way, framing them as a beautiful picture where devastation once existed. It was quite hot, and even though sweaty and uncomfortable, I didn't let the situation become a complaint.

It was very satisfying to get the pictures and be in the thick of the woods high above the village below. It was not only a feeling of accomplishment for the physical exertion it took but also the pride to have one more opportunity to be with Gaia's nature in this way.

I was soon distracted by the loud squawking of a hawk, and because the call was so loud, wondered what all the fuss was about. Or even more so, if a hawk was in pursuit of something to seize and eat, why it would be so obvious in calling attention to its whereabouts. The screeching was incessant as he flew high over my head to-and-fro, but was gliding at a speed above the tree tops that didn't allow me to get a closer look at him.

When the shrieking finally stopped, a deafening silence filled the air. Actively listening to the stillness, only moments had passed when I noticed a wisp of motion in my right peripheral vision. Turning to look, a huge Red Tail Hawk had made a landing in a pine tree and was swaying up and down as the branch tried to hold his weight.

Straining my eyesight to focus on this remarkable picture, it was shocking to see he was not more than fifty yards away.

Holding my breath for fear of making any sound that might startle him, I felt it impossible to make a split-second decision on grabbing my camera or just stand there staring in admiration. It was so wonderful and unexpected, I tried to do both, but just as the camera was in my hand, he bobbed once, twice, and on the third sway of the encumbered branch, lifted his wings in flight. I had gotten a good view of him anyway, and that was obviously the point.

This whole event took only seconds, and once I realized the loud, insistent calling had been for my benefit, the words followed. "Hey, see me? Get it? Look at me, I'm a hawk!" In another split second after feeling that flow, I knew Mr. Rock had given me evidence that he was indeed on the walk with me, just not in my pocket. He had wished to give me an eye-catching demonstration of his freedom and chosen way to journey. There are no words to really convey the joy derived from this experience other than to say I felt extremely blessed and like the luckiest person alive.

As I began my way back down the crags, amazement set in at how sweaty my hair and t-shirt had become, not to mention my fire red cheeks still flushed with overexertion from the climb up. Now was the time to cool off, breathe, and onward down the great cliff-like hill. Hawk called out again in the descent to lower levels that gave me an uncanny feeling I'd see him again near to where the hike began that day. And sure enough, there he was, circling high above the trees and dwellings a short distance from the beginning of the trailhead.

He was a glorious sight, and even though I didn't want to appear humanly greedy, sent out a thought request for him to make another landing to take his picture. But it never came to fruition because he was too busy showing off. That's OK; the camaraderie of such union replaced any feeling of a missed photo opportunity. He'd come one more time to emphasize his message, and there wasn't anything that could have minimized the thrill of the lesson learned that day as he spoke again. "You see, from the beginning of your walk is where I changed form and embodied myself as a hawk, journeying from start to finish with you, so it didn't matter where you put me."

His thoughts enforced the concept he'd given me earlier, and since I'd yearned in the past for a greater understanding of these matters, missing bits were clicking within me like puzzle pieces finding their match. Like flashing back to when I retrieved him on top of the post covered in bird poop desperate with worry I'd caused him harm when come to find out it was he who must have shat upon himself as a sign that he'd shifted form and become the bird. I just didn't get it at that moment, my human understanding had limited me.

All the many ways I'd been groomed as a human being to have specific thoughts and ideas about life had caused me to suffer. The woodland walk had released me from this restrictive thinking by opening my eyes to ways spirit can dash in and out of form. Even rock had the capability. What a relief to have memory restored that we are all shapeshifters, one with the all, and all with the one.

The experience enveloped sadness, and what took precedence was a feeling of being blessed with eternal peace. Back at the flat, I had placed Rock, Mr. Rock, Earthman, Keeper of the Forest, Pet Rock (he had many names) atop the TV while writing my story, occasionally looking at him in disbelief. I couldn't help but wonder if he was in his body at that moment or had gone elsewhere. At the risk of sounding too corny, I went ahead anyway and said out loud, "You Rock!"

Truth with No Proof

The Thirty-Six-Year-Old Wart

At sixteen years of age, I'd developed a wart on my foot between my big and second toe. A short time later, one also appeared on the back of my head above my pineal gland. Talk about above and below! My mother claimed the one on my foot was from wearing flip flops, and that the rubber divider had irritated my skin causing the discord. That wart got zapped and never came back. The one on my head was burnt off, received radiation treatment, and still returned.

It used to bug me, so I'd pick at it until it bled and be left with a sore spot on my head. Having to keep my hands off it until it healed and grew back into its crusty old self again became quite a cycle of self-abuse. Each time, I would promise myself to just stop it, but in no time the picking would start all over again. I suppose you could call this a form of self-mutilation with some obsessive-compulsive behavior added to the mix.

Many years later, I visited the doctor worried that irritating it all that time had caused a regeneration of cells and that something else may have developed. He didn't seem too worried, but when he said they could freeze-burn it off and hope it didn't come back, I decided against it. My theory was if it didn't work the first time when I was a teenager, it was best just to pass. In any case, it continued its progression until I was fifty-two years old. It was a great day when my niece who cut my hair on a regular basis said, "Oh, did you have the wart surgically removed Aunt Paula?" I gloated and replied, "No, I healed it myself." She didn't say a word, possibly dumbfounded from disbelief or confusion.

I had very casually reached for it one day and feeling the texture of it said to myself, "This is not the way of a Goddess, nor is it very flattering to be picking at a wart on my head…I am complete with this experience and I am choosing for it to shrivel up, dissipate, and have my scalp clear of this pimply malformation."

I wasn't upset or frustrated when I made this decree, but in truth, after some thirty-six years of picking at it had enough and felt it was time to stop. Calmly set into motion, it was still hard to believe that within two to three weeks, it had completely disappeared. I kept feeling the area, which was smooth without a trace of anything left behind.

I was encouraged after this incredible experience to take note of other disturbances regarding my physical body. Anything that hangs around my skin too long unnecessarily just gets a few taps with my finger, along with a silent decree for the issue to complete its cycle and clear. Many times, it works like magic, and then there have been instances where the problem lingered. In the case of the old wart-wash, I'll take a victory lap, and forever let it enrich my life knowing what can happen when you call upon your higher self for healing results.

Truth with No Proof

Psyche Surgery

One morning after jumping out of bed too quickly to get in the bathroom, I couldn't straighten myself up and fell to my knees in pain. Attempting to stand and stay upright was unbearable, so I crawled to my purse for some ibuprofen and dragged myself back into bed, desperate to find a position I could lie in without hurting.

Eventually, after moving very carefully for an hour along with some soft stretching, the situation improved. I'd never had such an episode before and knowing everything was about energy, scanned for other answers as to why my lower back had been aggravated above and beyond any other time. If there was an emotional link I wasn't aware, and if it was an arthritis flare-up, I was always grateful when the discomfort passed; however, this time it went way beyond that.

A great love of ice-skating as a young girl ended up with me sprawled on my back on the ice at times, which may have contributed to my body being affected this way. It would also ache badly after having stood for long periods of time in a stationary position, like the day after Thanksgiving meal preparations, or from standing in a long queue. These are the 3-D thoughts on what happened to my lower back and tailbone area. I was like a sitting duck anticipating a weather change until another realization unfolded.

What came to mind this unusually painful morning was a lifetime memory when I was with a group of people who were perceived by the community as a dangerous threat because of the spiritual abilities we possessed. The ruling council at the time decided the group would be spared and allowed to stay safely in the village if one of the group's members with the stronger abilities be done away with.

I was selected as the one to go and endured a very grisly death by being pulled in half just below the waist on a stretch board. I had literally and symbolically been *cut off* from the group. After having my life taken in such a heinous way, no wonder tailbone problems arose. Real dismemberment.

This is not shared to dwell on being a victim, but instead, put the focus on cellular memory in that part of my body. It reflected current life circumstances, where a similar theme of separating myself from someone I'd related to, activated the incredible stabbing pain at the base of my spine sharp enough to disable me.

There had been a recent disagreement with the man I was staying with after being attacked by him verbally. Not feeling safe in his home anymore, I left the next day, feeling the need to get as far away from him as possible and hopefully never see him again. Right or wrong, it was the motion of cutting myself off that seemed to be the trigger.

I thought back, and normally if a threat of any kind was perceived, I would just promptly remove myself from the situation. It never occurred to stay put and work things out, or even to double-check if what I sensed had been accurate. No, if it felt like a threat, it must be a threat, and off I went. If someone did something hurtful to me, I saw no reason to ever see them again. That is simply what made sense to me at the time, especially not knowing about past-life triggers. In some cases, the detachment was for my highest good, and then there were other instances where it'd been like cutting off one of my own limbs.

Even though in this case, the change of residence was for good reason, I still had anxiety producing thoughts about running into this man somewhere unexpectedly in the village. This got my attention because it was a state of nonfreedom. Something clicked within my psyche, realizing that if seeing him someplace did come to fruition, I could just politely say "hello" and carry on.

What a concept. No one would have that power over me again. I had been living in fear based energy of the past, and now was the time to integrate. No question, I'd done right by leaving a stressful residence, but it didn't mean I had to feel completely cut off from the situation. The simplicity of this revelation brought me an instantaneous sense of freedom.

I started soulfully speaking to my body about never needing to be separate from anyone or anything again. My choice was to fuse the tailbone area with self-love and self-care, no matter what the outside circumstances were. The basic premise was that me, my base chakra,[4] and tailbone area were one, and there was no need to continue creating conditions of separation within my body physical activated from memories of former times when the physical and emotional separation was an actual reality.[5]

Speaking to myself in a tender, reassuring voice that all these aspects could just be a part of me in wholeness, without

---

4. *Chakra* is a Sanskrit word for "wheel," translated to mean a point of physical or spiritual energy in the human body.
5. "Every particle of our physical body is imbued with the cellular memory of past-life experiences until otherwise transmuted or decoded by us. No judgment, it's just the way it is since everything is recorded by the body as if it were a storage device. The only way to delete its contents is for the energy residing there be allowed to uproot and surface. Once it is recognized and accepted for what it is, you can give it a hug and embrace the remnants of old memory in unconditional love. Your conscious care, and forgiveness (if needed), will impact any cell involved in past memory or coding, replacing traces of reactivity with neutralization."

fearful past reactivations, was powerfully healing because that kind of stabbing pain never occurred again. Yes, there were weather patterns and barometric pressure drops at various times that touched upon some of the arthritic vertebrae; however, they were only a faint ache compared to the day I fell to my knees in pain.

Everything, of course, cannot be attributable to lifetime memory, but it sure helps in alleviating the self-judgment of just being a crazy person who runs away from everything in life. Even though the body physical is the body physical, and it can feel scared, be sickened, and endure all sorts of problems, those effects will feel intensely magnified when there is an added spiritual component of past-life cellular memory.

There is so much more than meets the eye in terms of our third-dimensional discernment and the societal rules and regulations we judge ourselves and our behavior by.

Truth with No Proof

Shaky Knees

What other reason could there be for feeling like my knees were buckling at the sight of my new sister-in-law? Not just weak knees, I would literally start to tremble like I was about to drop. It didn't make sense in plain terms because I had just married this woman's husband's brother, and as a new family member, there was no previous history to warrant such a reaction. Not in this lifetime anyway.

I had gone to a sensitive and her specialty was reading past lives. She clairvoyantly saw a lifetime with my new family members, where there was an old betrayal involving my current sister-in-law. We had been friends, when she very suddenly turned on me by literally sticking a knife in my back—hence, the feeling of dropping to my knees.

Upon hearing this scenario, a resonance of truth vibrated throughout my whole being, and the sensation of shakiness in my body never occurred again. The pure acknowledgment of betrayal surfacing helped my conscious mind embrace that aspect of lifetime memory into wholeness.

In a new now, my physical body understood what had happened between us, allowing me to start fresh, without the urgent feeling to run away every time I saw her.

Truth with No Proof

The Death of a Dead Man

After our second meeting, it became clear this was someone I'd known previously. As I was saying good-bye and walking out the door, the name of who he'd been in our last lifetime together was dropped into my ear. He was very well-known, and cellular memory ignited as I remembered helping him to realize his strengths by supporting all his endeavors, so it was natural to have the same admiration as I connected with his essence in the current life. The automatic tendency to benefactor his talents and many spiritual gifts some thousand years later brought a familiar feeling of joy and satisfaction. For a short period of time anyway.

Much to my chagrin, the admiration I had carried for him was not warranted in the present. Just because you've had a glorious past life with someone doesn't necessarily mean it will be that way next time around. We had been spending a lot of time together, when suddenly he started speaking to me in a very insulting and demeaning way. What? It was like being with someone who had a split personality disorder, and even though he had a sweet side and was fun to be with, you never knew when the emotional climate would drastically change.

It was startling, and I don't suppose it helps matters much

that he also had a penchant for drinking whiskey, which wasn't complementary to his authentic self. Once or twice, you think maybe the erratic behavior was attributable to just having a bad day, but after several bouts of unexplainable temper tantrums, you begin to wonder.

The last time he'd downloaded a wealth of hostility, I left the space with the understanding I'd return periodically to see if he had come back to himself, mentioning that if nothing shifted, I'd have to remove myself completely. In that instance, after my second return visit he had softened, mellowed, and was apologetic, so this allowed us to continue onward.

Like a roller-coaster ride of ups and downs, you're never quite sure if or when the lurking monster will appear again, so you pray, keep your fingers crossed, and hope for the best. But walking on eggshells is no fun either. The spontaneous and unwarranted outbursts of aggression were unmistakable signs that something was wrong. Personality or mental issues, maybe even bipolar in combination with alcohol abuse? I wasn't sure, and not wanting to be judgmental, was willing to just hold space for him.

There were times when he could be calm and clear, and we often worked together as a team to utilize our spiritual gifts via the laying on of hands for people. We had rented a small space for this purpose, paying special attention to creating a pristine and peaceful environment. We were preparing to start the day, when he became irritated about why I needed to take the trash out, and that it wasn't important, and no one cared anyway.

This was noticeably out of context since he was there with me to see people who had healing appointments, and we'd just tidied the room and offered up a prayer for everyone's highest good. And then wham! Out came the troll. I quickly did what I could to avoid further confrontation to keep the space energetically in flow for the clients.

The ability to turn on me so quickly could no longer be ignored, and I knew that even though I had his back, it became crystal clear that for whatever reason, he did not have mine. It was confusing because he had such a strong ability as a healer and could be very empathic, yet two seconds later, act like a sociopath who cared less about anyone or anything.

I tried to make excuses hoping he'd shake off this incorrigible aspect of himself once and for all, but no perception of mine seemed to help or make a difference. It wasn't worth the turmoil and was depleting my energy always trying to figure out where the gloom came from or why, so I made the choice to let go of the friendship. Without the fullness of graphic details, the last round of aggressive speech toward me had been enough. If it were all bad, you'd just leave without hesitation; however, it wasn't, which filled the situation with a duality of conflicting feelings that created confusion.

For example, there was a time when I became very congested with cold-like symptoms, and he worried I'd developed allergies and proceeded to clean my flat from top to bottom hoping the removal of dust would improve how I was feeling. These moments were dearly appreciated.

In his youth, he'd gotten in trouble landing him in jail, but even though incarcerated, his good side came out because he did what he could to help the other inmates by writing letters for those who couldn't write English on their own. Helping the underdog was an asset of his.

Sadly, he witnessed some horrific fights during his time there in which several inmates were murdered. He'd been beaten badly himself in one of these scrimmages but after that managed to stay clear of future poundings. When it was time for his release, the warden added he was one of the best inmates they'd ever seen, and everyone upon his departure waved from the windows of the institution to give him a heartfelt send-off. This meant a lot being it was in a different country, and he was so far from home.

And so onward with life, except for one little problem.

When he left prison, he didn't leave alone. His compassionate nature extended out beyond the call of duty when he'd allowed one of these blokes who'd been murdered to attach themselves to his auric body. This was some thirty years prior to our meeting, and he had allowed spirit attachment from this discarnate entity for so long, it was hard to know when he was being himself in his own body, or when his unseen mate was playing the part.

What I do know is when his astral (the realm closest to earth) buddy stepped in was when things ran amuck quickly and he became aggressive, uncaring, and all the opposite attributes of his true nature took control. Not something we grow up discussing, so it's the last thing you'd imagine; however, that was what happened. I had anchored much love and light during our friendship, and eventually this discarnate could no longer affix himself to the same extent of the previous bonding and had to release. He had to let go. That was the good news.

The not-so-good news was when he found his way to me one night as I slept, taunting me by shaking my arm with a menacing laugh to upset me. This restless soul had been very content living close to earth in the astral realm and had no intention of moving on, so he felt revengeful because I had caused a disruption in his undercover living arrangement.

Truth with No Proof

Being a medium, I'd had some previous experiences with discarnate entities and rescue work for those who get temporarily lost or wayward due to suicide and sudden or traumatic passing, but nothing like this. I was afraid to breathe. But only a nanosecond passed when I heard a loud noise like a jumbo 747 arriving, and within seconds, peace and calm were restored to my orbit.

One of my guides, guardians, or sentinels perceived what was going on and stepped in immediately to assist by removing the entity from my field. He hadn't wanted to go on his own, and any polite talk suggesting he move on to the other side was to no avail—but whoever showed up on my behalf wasted no time, he was given no say-so in the matter and was ousted! Thank God and all that's holy.

It reminded me of the many times I've felt someone who had passed hanging about the earth plane because they got confused or weren't sure what happened so they need a little talking to or reassurance and often happily accept the guidance and move into the light, but no, not this dude—thirty some years he hung out and lived vicariously through my friend who he influenced with his attitudes and beliefs often.

In the old days, they'd just call a priest to conduct an exorcism and hope it worked. Even so, this was a tough nut to crack. It was shocking for many reasons, and how grateful am I that help showed up so quickly. I'd never been frightened with my experiences with spirit, even having contact with some of the angry or unhappy ones expressing in the darkness, but this was something else. It certainly is not shared to frighten anyone but more to reiterate we are all guided and have an angel who watches over us, which has been demonstrated to me time and time again.

The sad thing is my friend was awakened, and he knew on some level what was occurring and allowed it anyway, and for so long, the guy in a way had taken him over, which hardly ever happens here. Usually, a sensitive person will become aware someone is hanging around and quickly tell them they must go, but not in this case, he permitted it. To his complete detriment though, because he'd shared many times about all his broken relationships and family estrangement and complained about being left alone in every instance. And of course, according to his version of the story, it was always everyone else's fault.

Well frankly, I don't know after my short time of companionship with him who could put up with it for five minutes. The discarnate being was not the friendly sort and got rid of anyone who felt like a threat to his ethereal survival since his main objective was to stay good and attached. I'd been strong enough to pull his cover by standing up for what was fair and righteous, so he attempted to come and bully me. But it didn't work, whether I'd been completely conscious of my spiritual maneuvering or not, he messed with the wrong fraulein. The tables were turned quickly sending him back to the dimension where he belonged.

And then there is the matter of a person being willing to look at themselves, their own personal history, and take an inventory if need be to keep their own personal house in order. Or if something is not right, at the very least, do some investigative work on your own behalf and strive to rectify it.

It was sad, because anytime I attempted to discuss this or help him figure out why he was misaligned, it fell upon deaf ears, and he'd only say I was at fault and being problematic for wanting to argue with him. If pushed, he would apologize saying he was an asshole, but the sentiments of being "sorry" were cosmetic and very short-lived. Soon, the whole scenario would simply repeat itself, which is what happens when someone is unwilling to take any responsibility for their behavior or actions.

Very warped, so clearly, I couldn't assist even if I wanted to. I don't know whatever happened to him or how he must have felt without his invisible sidekick influencing his speech and actions, and it doesn't really matter because my involvement with them both is complete.

Early on in our conversations, I noticed he'd always say "we" when referencing himself like he wasn't alone. If I'd suggest something to do, for example, his reply was, "We will wait to hear from you then." I thought it was cute and perhaps his own special way to include his guide, angel, or spirit helpers. How naïve was I? Truth be known, I can only share it now to possibly assist someone else. That is how I turn the experience into a win.

The main thing is the one who had passed over was stopped dead in his tracks (no pun intended) from lingering on the earth plane and put in his proper place in the afterlife where he belonged. I understand you will go to whatever dimension best matches your consciousness at the time you pass, so I can only imagine, and trust, he was delivered unto the space he deserved and was meant to be in.

Good to remember that each time a person reincarnates, they come with a unique personality and set of circumstances, all precisely matched and geared toward what they've chosen to experience on earth. The reason for incarnating may be entirely different from their last earthly walk, and free will is always in play, so they may appear a completely different version of the person you knew last time you were in human form together. This perception can assist in lessening the effect of hurt feelings from heartache and disappointment.

The moral of the story is if you have someone unusually unruly or out of whack in your life, there could be reasons for it other than depression, alcoholism, drug addiction, and or mental illness.

Athena

I was taking in all the wonders of the Louvre Museum in Paris, when I saw the immense and incredible 40 ft. high statue of Athena. With a tone of detachment, I thought, "Is it big enough?" An important figure in Greek mythology, Athena, was close to my heart for many reasons, and yet upon seeing this fantastic replica of her was only aware of my dry sarcasm. Not really knowing the full story on what happened to the original *Athena Parthenos*, didn't seem important at the time.

Years later, contemplating in meditation where to travel for my next excursion I was impressed with, "Try Athens." And so it was. Already overseas, utilizing a time-share week made the arrangements to visit Athens much less complicated. The strange part was after the departure from Birmingham, England, I started to cry as we got closer to Greece but didn't know why.

Seemed like such an odd reaction compared to the excitement that normally preceded visiting a place I'd never been before. It felt like something remarkably significant was about to unfold but didn't have a clue on what it might be. I had much resonance to Greek mythology and was looking forward to being in the home of so many Olympians.

Once at the hotel, I began looking at maps trying to contain the eagerness to be everywhere at once. Finally, deciding my first stop would be the Parthenon, the excitement was building to see this temple built by the Athenians in honor of their beloved Athena and feel the majesty of it all. As I arrived in Attica and started the climb toward where the central temple resided, tears started to fall again, only this time it progressed into a full sob. Interesting experience when you startle yourself; however, focused on reaching the summit where all the history unfolded, I trekked on.

Reading the signposts through blurred teary vision was no easy task, and the added strain of only a few of them being referenced in English created a challenge, but I managed to collect enough information to paint a picture of the history and changes that had occurred over the course of time high up on the altar shrine. Once, up above the city, I raced around to all the adjacent structures savoring the best for last, imagining how regal Athena might appear when I reached the temple that housed her statue.

When I finally figured out where her place of glory was and stood before the monument, no Athena! I didn't realize in the search that she wasn't even there. In fact, hadn't been there since the fifth century AD when, according to theory, she was removed, stolen, or destroyed. No wonder I was crying, my heart ached, wishing for Athena to be home with her people on her perch above Athens. I was amazed at my naïveté and lack of historical facts. I truly thought she'd be there when 90 percent of the tourists visiting probably already knew she was not.

From the time of my visit to the Louvre, up till the Athens trip, more lifetime memory had been revealed regarding my connections to the Goddess of Wisdom and her Owl, which is why there was so much more emotion flooding through me. Every cell in my body had felt Athena's Temple was missing Athena, hence the tears. My personality just didn't get it, but the rest of me did, which is why the crying started on the plane ride headed toward Greece and reached a crescendo climbing the stairs to the Parthenon.

Based on the depth of feeling, I couldn't help but wonder if when I originally saw her likeness in Paris, if her full essence was nowhere near the statue due to it being a copy—and her spirit just stayed atop the hill at the Parthenon, where she rightfully belonged. This might explain why the replica of her at the museum had felt ostentatious and empty because, without her energy, all that remained was a vacant sculpture.

Thinking had never done much to help the cause, but for this purpose, I'll never know for certain. It was proof enough that the missing link of past-life memory was exposed after reliving a dearly connected truth. There was no need for that cellular memory to remain embedded deep in sleep; it only asked for my acknowledgment, so I'd no longer weep.

Hitting the Skids

I couldn't stop crying. All the important things in life had just toppled, and with no place to go felt lost in space. My heart was heavy with the weight of shattered dreams, and not knowing what to do next, hoped to escape the constraints of time by just going for a walk.

There were some great hills in the area, and as I started the climb upward with an unhappy me, myself, and I, trudged along very sluggishly from carrying the burden of broken human relationships. Containing the energy of it all in the silver locket hanging over my heart was symbolic in keeping my thoughts from traveling. My choice was just to hold the energy of these heartaches to myself for process and healing. The energy swarmed me like a pack of bees, and losing my step, almost took a great stumble.

Almost falling hard on my butt, I heard the objective voice of my guide say, "Can you get to the top?" I answered silently, "Yeah sure I can," thinking if I did fall, I'd just get right back up and continue. There must have been a little fight left in me. Bittersweet though, because all of life had felt like a competition to see who can get to the top first. Next, I hear, "So, when you get to the top, you'll realize, you'll know, that the fall was just part of the journey up." Lights on! I realized all I had to do was keep focused on reaching my destination, and the number of falls or how long it took to get there was irrelevant.

After dwelling in the dimness of devastation, this was a welcome shift in my emotional climate after hearing those plain but terrifically healing words.[6] In the new light, drama and trauma seemed like things of the past, and moments later, this proclamation manifested in the sound of music. Looking around, it was hard to imagine where it would be coming from in the middle of the high desert with only hills and dirt roads around for miles.

After much consternation, the answer came. The sound was coming from the wind blowing through iron pipes in the ground. Hollow, and yet richly embellished. An ancient symphony of notes produced a whistle that mimicked a Celtic flute with the professional quality you'd expect from a recording studio. But it was only the barren landscape singing this song

---

[6]. "All the breaths that feel like a failure, and all the breaths that feel like a win, together, they put Humpty back together again. Mention of this little nursery rhyme is how I bring balance to the old paradigm story on this planet where when you're down, you're down and may feel too broken to get up and live again. You beat yourselves up so badly for falling, you cannot even think about how to mend the wounds, the overwhelming of such feelings keeps you flat on the ground. The new paradigm concept that whisks us all into ascension light—the breaths that feel like a win, the breaths that feel like a sin—they all blend into one breath anyway: the breath of love." From Paula and Ascended Master Kuthumi, *Love Is Enough* (LuLu.com, 2012).

that echoed eternity. And in my vision, I'm quite sure I saw the face of father time fall away, and in a twinkling configuration of sparkling white lights, infinity took his place.

Truth with No Proof

Cursing a Blue Streak

I knew the day would be brutal if I didn't take it easy because everything I touched would either fall out of my hand or involve some clumsy movement on my part that would aggravate me to the point of cursing. Butterfingers! My goal that morning was to go for a ride but started fumbling around out in the tack room too, dropping my saddle, and then the reins, and before long, the worst language I have ever heard poured through me like liquid tar.

Wow, never speaking like this, I wondered where the words were coming from. Even though somewhat consciously aware that I needed to avoid rushing to avoid catastrophe, every time something didn't go my way, which was about every couple of minutes, a few obscene words would roll through my mind like a runaway train. Now, everything and everyone was a _____! In the atmosphere of such rage, I quickly reminded myself to be very gentle with the horses.

This saved the day because as soon as one of them wanted to put their head down to eat the green grass below, my first inclination was to scream, swear, and give a swat with the rope. I was grateful to have the presence of mind to collect the thought and say to myself, "Oh, lots of energy on the planet today sister, go easy." Also, in that moment, I wondered what other people did when they perceived such energy and acted out by assaulting anyone or anything within arm shot. It wasn't hard to understand why the news was filled with reports of violence and acts of assault.

Approximately five minutes had passed, when I decided it wasn't worth all the fuss and decided to go back in the house and just forget it. I paused. But that wasn't my choice either. I hadn't gotten to ride all week and was really looking forward to it, so to abandon the plan would have felt like defeat by allowing this crappy energy to ruin my day. I slowed my roll, continued to tack up, and was ready to walk off the property.

Even though I had cursed a blue streak and grappled with impatience, I held the mind space for remembering there is no energy on this earth plane that is taller, or bigger than *I am*. (as taught to me by my guide) The more I acknowledged that my choice was to go calmly, be gentle with myself and the horses, and come back to my home safe and sound, the more the ride flowed in accord with my intention.

Feeling the vulnerability of it, I sent out a silent prayer for all of humankind and the animal kingdom as well, for I could only imagine based on my experience what someone else might have done when caught up in so much anger, rage, and hostility with no tools or awareness on how to handle such aggression. It could have turned out to be a ride from hell had I not reined in the energy.

My horses were happily eating their hay and had been given carrots as a treat for putting up with me, so they were content. The satisfaction was going on the ride without canceling my plans due to faulty energy; likened to faulty weather, they both come in on you quickly with no advanced warning. I wasn't sure what was going on but knew this amount of hostility flooding my aura had to be coming from somewhere.

First on the investigative list of possible explanations was to check the news page on my computer. Right away, a picture of President Bush came into view with a caption announcing that it was the one-year anniversary date of the Iraqi War. Who knew? Looks like I did. In my reality, it mattered not whether I got the warfare thoughts of those involved that very day a year ago, or perceived people's reactivity opening their morning newspapers to see this anniversary reminder.

The success was not battering myself, or anyone else by getting sucked in. Regrettably, there had been times when I reacted, screamed, took a slap at somebody, or spoke harsh words to the point of hurting feelings. This time I knew it was outside energy and caught the monkey before it wrangled me.

It was great to have recognized the potential pitfall and just step over it without falling in. Holding the vibration of love is a highly specialized job,[7] especially when you feel continually impressed by energies that do not represent love.

---

[7]. "I know it may seem hard to believe, especially when many lightworkers have let out a sigh at the amount of anger and aggression expressed in the world, and they feel hopeless to know how to possibly balance that which has spiraled out of control. One breath at a time, dear ones, is how to align any misgiving and keep it a brief encounter. Finally, a brush with hostility can either ruin your day as you fall into a murky swamp of energy that influences everything you do and say, or on the other hand, keep any unpleasant experience short-lived by remembering that feelings of fear or anger can be aligned in a single breath. It's the moment it takes to direct this awareness as you inhale "In you go, fear," as if you're a magical oven, and the heat of you fires it into love on the next exhale." From Paula, *Inspired by Lord Buddha, One Defining Moment* (Amazon Kindle, 2015).

Feeling Like a Failure

Marius, under normal circumstances, was a fair and reasonable man, so most of the screaming and yelling must have been the hurt expressing for me calling the marriage over, which seemed to throw reasonability out the window. It was a daily constant fight to even speak of the most mundane matters, so I was gearing up for the task at hand, which was to be reasonable myself when everything else fell apart. It all came crashing in at the same time.

The lawyer I selected to represent me attempted to speak with my soon-to-be ex-husband, but because of his thick accent and belligerence, the call was cut short and the simple matter at hand never got resolved.

I knew something as important as my settlement after seventeen years of marriage would most likely take years to resolve at this rate. That was the only call ever made by the attorney because the thought of paying for these ongoing verbal standoffs, not to mention the indecency of putting my abundance in someone else's hand to manage was unthinkable.

The very week Marius and I were to negotiate our final

divorce settlement, my car broke down, and a day later, my laptop crashed. Even though these items could be fixed, it was mustering up the strength to deal with already feeling crushed under everyday stress, when boom, another battle would present adding to the intensity.

The lawyer I was so certain could help didn't seem able to do anything in the presence of Marius's booming voice, and the few remaining things needed to keep myself going had all just broken down. It was too much, and the worst feeling, that after much praying for assistance, I had somehow misunderstood the guidance received and picked the wrong person to handle my legal matters.

I was trying hard to maintain my dignity but felt ravaged on the battleground of life. I looked like a Halloween costume of walking death, with a scrunched-up face and bones poking out everywhere. I felt like a failure and couldn't help but feel like my guide had let me down.

A few weeks later, after riding the emotional roller coaster of being upset at everyone and everything, I heard a clairaudient whisper, "Samuel, the prophet. Samuel." This was a strange and unusual thing to hear, but it got my attention, and upon looking it up as I always did when hearing something in my ear, found out that Samuel felt like a failure too.

I was intrigued and read on. Things hadn't gone well for him either, and certainly not what he expected, especially when he followed and honored the guidance he had received to the best of his ability, but still was not understanding what went wrong or why. There was a similar thread because he and I both wished so much for a positive outcome in a situation and the feeling when it doesn't go that way because the result is dependent on another person's free will.

Samuel was the last of the judges to rule Israel. He was also the first prophet in the line of prophets who stood outside the role of leader to serve as a conscience of the king. As a prophet, he seemed to have a special connection. He heard the voice of God in ways that most of the people couldn't, and he was given messages to pass on to individuals. However, Samuel's career took a turn like none of the others.

Israel had been a loose federation of tribes held together by a common ancestry and ruled sporadically by judges who rose to power among them. During Samuel's life, God shifted Israel's political system to that of a monarchy, in which a king and his descendants ruled over the whole nation, drew support from all the tribes, and had the power to raise an army from all those tribes.

For Samuel's own life, these changes must have been

difficult. He had no pattern from Israel's earlier history to follow. Another personal difficulty was that Samuel was passing off his own power to someone else. His own sons were not men after God's heart as Samuel had been, and so he was unwilling to turn the power over to them. Instead, he had to wait on God to show him whom to select as king. Things didn't get much easier once Saul became king. It turned out that power went to Saul's head, and he began to act like he could do whatever he wanted.

Imagine how hard it must have been for Samuel to go to the person he had thought would be the beginning of a long line of kings and to tell him and all Israel that God was rejecting him and choosing someone else. It must have felt a little bit like Samuel himself had failed, and he must have been a little afraid of Saul's power as king. Nevertheless, Samuel followed God through these uncharted waters and eventually named David, a man after God's own heart, to be king in Israel.

Making big changes is never easy. Bringing bad news to people is never easy. Turning your power over to someone else is never easy. Admitting that things did not turn out as expected is never easy. Samuel experienced them all. He must have had many sleepless nights, many days of confusion and uneasiness, but when it was all over, he and all of Israel came through the transition well.

Managing to come through my own transitions, I realized you can never look too hard at the present circumstances or at the unknowns of the future, because you may lose all hope. Not a worse feeling than that. This piece of guidance regarding Samuel's life gave me comfort, and that I didn't need to feel so let down by the lawyer I'd been guided too. When all was said, and done, even though matters were very dragged out by his office and most of the negotiating done by me, the job got completed.

I knew that God and my guides still loved and cared about me. All this from hearing that one little phrase, "Samuel the prophet."

Truth with No Proof

Lady in the Hospital

For the longest time, I'd only offering my healing services to animals, mostly because they didn't judge, demand results, or have a skeptical attitude. They just sensed I had something to offer and would gravitate toward me in a very natural way. Quite often, even animals who were shy or afraid of strangers would come over without reservation, plopping right down on my foot to let me know they would like some energy. They were always appreciative, so it was joyful to be of assistance.

I was amazed at the results, and over time, eventually worked up the confidence to lay my hands on people, which also produced encouraging results. Some might say after a session that they started getting a good night's sleep for the first time in twenty years, or report chronic pain had gone away. I'd always hoped for miraculous cures and fixes, but well-meaning as it sounded, had to put my ego aside and trust that my prayer to be of service would be helpful, even if there wasn't a noticeable outcome.

Sometimes the results were physical, and many times spiritual, which since they both work together for a person's highest good, anything and everything was wonderful. A cure could be a simple perception change that eases how a person thinks and feels about things, alleviating phobia, worry, and anxiety.

Word spread through the grapevine, and I'd answered a call to visit a lady who'd been hospitalized in a weakened condition from cancer. I had gone for a visit to see if I could bring comfort and found her in a very timid and frail condition. She agreed to my offering of "laying on of hands" as I found myself impressed to rest my palms gently over her ankles and feet.

Moments later, I became aware of a presence standing directly behind her bed where she laid her head on the pillow. I was speechless when I looked up and saw Jesus![8] Silenced by utter shock, I kept it to myself. It was enough for me to digest, let alone risking her thinking I was some crackpot conjuring up visions to aid my cause like a circus act.

Within seconds, Jesus had motioned me to throw him some of the discordant energy I had collected in my hands from her body. A fluid and very natural flow began, where I imagined

---

8. "It was not meant to create another idol for you to worship as a statue upon a pedestal, or to show you that the power was delegated only to a few of God's favorites. The example was given to you not only for the *show*, but also for all of you—God's sentient sons and daughters—to recognize the likeness, and have the realization that you could be the same. The role model was offered not for something to adore, as much as to remind you of the equal opportunity you all have, to make use of your same inherit potential as shown by Jesus, or any of your other great teachers who have walked on earth. You are it all anyway, if one of you has stepped forth to show in the public eye, it has only been to demonstrate it is possible for everyone." From Paula and Ascended Master Kuthumi, *Love Is Enough* (LuLu.com, 2012).

myself rolling the energy in a ball and tossing it to him, at which time, he rolled the energy around in his hands and tossed it back to me. I then directed this blessed and transmuted energy return into her system by laying my hands on again. Back and forth it went like a game of catch. What an honor!

I had sensed there was a twofold reason for his visit that day. Obviously, he loved this lady dearly, and second, he wanted to remind me what he had taught me about working with energy two thousand years earlier. Boy, was I reminded. Never forgot it, and my mode of delivering healing frequencies shifted dramatically from that moment forward, including all the expanded memories of how I could move, shape, and shift any type of energy. I completed the visit with a gentle heartfelt pat on her feet, and a verbal prayer request for an improvement in how she was feeling.

I got a call from the lady's dear friend, who had initially set up the appointment to say that she had gone home from the hospital several days later and was fine. In fact, feeling fine had merged into a full remission. That was the last I heard, and way God enough for me.

Truth with No Proof

Mary Comes Alive

I was traveling in a European city known well for its spectacular cathedrals and opera houses, and even though English was not the primary language, some of the historical markers and signs had an English translation, which made it more fun to have the full picture. After finding a very–old-looking cathedral on a side street, and taking some photos of the dramatic exterior, I went inside to explore. The baroque elegance was a sight to behold and at the same time an overwhelming major theme of male dominance throughout. The pictures, statues, and plaques were all masculine images.

I often wondered when visiting these sites, why more females had not risen to the same religious fame as the men. I gave my honoring and acknowledged the reverence they'd incited just the same, but as I was about to exit, noticed a side enclave hidden to the rest of the massive masculine archways and scurried over to see what I had missed. A beautiful statue of Mother Mary on an altar with prayer books laid at her feet where people had written their prayer requests. The little room was filled with tender feeling.

It was a welcome and lovely sight. I lit a candle at the small worship box and wrote a message in the open prayer book, not to request anything, but a simple, appreciative, thank-you to Mary for being the representation of a female master. After glancing at the books full of prayers, I couldn't imagine how anyone could possibly answer them all. They contained line after line of names for those who were suffering, ill, or in a state of grief.

In a way, it was great folks had a place to come and lay it all down, and in another way, completely overwhelming at how to soothe the suffering from a human point of view. I left feeling quite satisfied that within this giant magnitude of a home for Jesus and male constituents, was also a little room for Mary. The feminine was present, even if ushered off to a far corner in a hidden back wing, the mother had been recognized.

The friend who accompanied me on this journey was exploring other parts of the city, and we met up a bit later in the central square to go on to a mutual point of interest. We were racing to be on time for a special showing zipping through back alleys to reach our destination, when we ran into a woman on a back staircase of the train station. She was carrying two heavy bags that slowed her stride up the stairs. I offered to help carry them, but she held her focus on just methodically plodding up the stairwell.

Eventually, we all reached the platform area and were just

standing there, when she came over and started speaking to me in a different language. Offering again, in broken spurts of English to help her with the bags using hand and arm gestures, left me quite certain she knew what I meant. She politely ignored it though and just kept talking. Not wanting to be rude, I'd occasionally nod my head to participate in the conversation even though I didn't understand a word she was saying.

My friend looked on rather astonished, when suddenly the woman's words transitioned into clear spoken English. You could only shake your head, or stand there in awe with your mouth hanging open. I mean there was no broken English in this transition from full-on foreign tongue, to clear, smooth-spoken English! Knowing this was an extraordinary event, I was grateful to have had a witness, and at the same time, reached for understanding on what it all meant.

Looking back, I could only remember something about her brother owning a bookstore and that he was getting married. I could not recall what else was said and to this day have not made sense of what I did remember. The foreign language suddenly becoming clear, spoken English gave me amnesia like I'd received a bump on my head that joggled my brains.

She asked where we were going, and I expressed my excitement about attending a special horse show and demonstration. We finally dashed off and continued in a hurry once the realization set in that the unusual encounter had ended. I looked back to see the lady walking away, carrying the heavy bags like a seasoned veteran with one balanced in each hand. We gleefully skipped ahead in a whirlwind of activity, sight-seeing, and many other blessed things to partake of.

It wasn't until a day later the thought occurred to me that I had received a special visit from an ascended master. Mary had heard me express my thankfulness in the little chapel designated to her at the cathedral the previous day and came to give a hello. The heavy bags she carried left me impressed with the clarity that they were a representation of the prayer books that laid on the altar at church; they were sacred to her, and so she held them close. It was a silent but poignant way to show each prayer was very important, so she read and answered every one of them.

She wished to convey that the weight of so many prayers meant no hardship to her. I was humbled, as I could not imagine in my humanness ever being able to address the weight of concerns in those bags without a single complaint. It's difficult to express the fullness of the feeling, and yet it was clear to me the woman we met on the street had been a channel for Mary to pop in and say hello.[9]

It seemed rather grandiose to think a being of her stature would come down from the heavens to speak to me. Seems like a stretch when you've been brought up to believe the saints and masters are so much higher and mightier than you. Yet, on the other hand, my guide told me these masters that have been worshipped high upon the statue bases they stand upon, were meant as living examples to show we can attain mastery and be the same. I can only pray to live up to such elegance.

---

9. "As masters in the ascended state, we can come and go as we choose, and that may include making appearances on earth in a physical body for several minutes, or for an extended amount of time if so impressed. We dearly love humanity, and will either take human form ourselves to bring assistance, or give someone else a nonphysical nudge to deliver a message we wish to impart. In the case of master manifesting on earth, we will take on a very ordinary appearance to blend in the general background with ease, so not to frighten or startle you in any way." From Paula, *Inspired by Lord Buddha, One Defining Moment* (Amazon Kindle, 2015).

Truth with No Proof

Purple Light in the Bush

I would talk to my master guide, Saint Germain, with the faith, hope, and trust that he could hear me. There wasn't really anyone to share my deepest feelings with about my soul journey, and since my best friend was ten thousand miles away, I'd share with him. He was my best friend on the other side of life, and I was very thankful for his guidance and watchful eye.

Many years previously, I was lucky enough to find out he was my guide through a person (Sara) who was a channel for ascended masters, and ever since then, consciously spent time cultivating my connectedness to him. He is known as Ascended Master Saint Germain and seen in photographs wearing a rich purple cape and Maltese Cross pendant, which was identifiably his trademark along with being known as "keeper of the violet flame."

I've received many signs and guideposts along the way that it was this being on the purple ray who guides me. It wasn't like I heard this information and just adopted it blindly; there were many indications and other rings of truth in a third-dimensional sense that nurtured acceptance and catapulted me into the arms of truth with no proof. Still, it didn't rule out the times my very active imagination accused me of making it all up, so on those bad-hair days, I just accepted it as a tender part of being human.

Thinking back of my innocence as a young schoolgirl picking a violet-color graduation dress long before the significance of that color was known to me was a key. It unlocked a remembrance not forgotten, especially since there had been hundreds of various colored dresses to look at. A small but powerfully resonant memory as such heightened the meaning of it all and bolstered my sense of trust in present time.

One of his previous incarnations on earth was as the father of Jesus, so he is also known as Joseph. Even though I was brought up Catholic, my love for Mary and Jesus went far beyond anything you could attribute to education.

Walking home from elementary school one day while crying my eyes out at the thought of how much I loved Jesus and his family was another indication. These tears were proof of something other than being enraptured by the sentiment of religious training or an attempted brainwashing conspiracy. There was a deeper truth of a love that, even at a young age, defied needing proof, and whose depth could only be described as profoundly heart-held.

I would speak to Joseph or Saint Germain telepathically about things that worried me, things that pleased me, or any of the above. The ascension process was not something you could speak to the average person on the street without them thinking you were a bit loopy. Even my closest circle of friends over the years who were of like mind would get a bit bored with the same repeated topic discursive. It was grandly important to me, so rather than hold it all inward, I'd speak to Saint Germain.

Admiring the greenery as I walked on a familiar pathway always mesmerized by Gaia's beauty, I was within reach of my camera. Having photos of nature to enjoy always provided inspiration and encouragement in the days ahead when there might not be much else to uplift the spirit.

Taking shots as I walked, I said to Saint Germain, "You know, if there were a book entitled *I Love the Earth*, I wonder how many people would buy it." It didn't seem to me that people talked much about earth's magnificence unless watching a documentary on TV, so it wasn't spoken of very often, and that felt amiss to me.

I already knew I could speak to those on the spirit side of life, but I was sharing with him telepathically how wonderful it would be to have someone here on earth who loved Gaia as much as I did to speak with.

My communication felt as gentle as the Scottish mist. There was a reprieve in the sky fall as I took a picture of the glistening dew on a plant and the way it mixed with a spider's web. How delicately the moisture held on such a sublime surface. As my flash went off, I caught a glimpse of a purple light and thought I might be seeing things. I quickly looked for the review button on my camera to do a double take. Sure enough, there was a bright purple light in the bush!

When I got home and downloaded the pictures on my laptop, there was a sequence of four shots that showed a progression of a faint white light; then a very bright white light above the plant with shades of violet or purple just below; followed by a full-on purple dome of light over half of the plant; and lastly, the white and purple tones fading away. I couldn't believe it, but I could believe it.

Here I had been rambling on to the keeper of the violet flame about wishing for someone to talk to about ascension and my love of the earth, and it must have been his way to say, "Ah, excuse me, what am I chopped liver? You are talking to someone who loves the earth as much as you do." Oops, Saint Germain had heard every word I said.

Feeling dumbfounded and a bit sheepish for any hint of doubt that he was anything other than omnipresent, I vowed very consciously never to take my relationship with him for granted again. For the most part, I believe with all my heart that he hears me, and then, when he gives me black-and-white proof like the instantaneous visual confirmation via purple light appearing out of nowhere, I'm left a bit dazed. Must be due to all the former training and conditioning of needing proof for a matter to be believable.

Let's face it: even though we pray, or speak to those on the other side, it's always nice to have some form of validation when dealing with the unseen. Otherwise, you could easily vanquish any of these notions into the realm of nothingness.

What a glorious happening when you do get a spontaneous gift, reflecting that your very existence is sustained by the love of God and the guides and guardians God has appointed you. Like the miracle of seeing water droplets delicately dangle from the spider's web, my eyes welled with tears of gratitude for being reminded that as much as it can feel that way at times, I am never truly alone.

Truth with No Proof

Tag Team Seals

Walking on the stony sand beach with the tide out, I noticed the head of what looked like a big dog swimming and felt upset someone's pet might be lost. Another few blinks revealed a seal popping his head up and out of the water to check me out. With no one around for miles, it was eerily quiet and wondered if it was the vibration of my footsteps along the shoreline that alerted him to my presence.

It was diving in and out of the water with little leaps in the air that clarified for me this was no dog. Being from Wisconsin, I could spot a cow a mile away, but the Isle of Man and surrounding Irish Sea was new territory for me. He would come around often, making it one of my favorite places to walk, and I always looked forward to seeing that friendly marvelous head bob in and out of the water.

Heading to my magical cove on a unique mission that weekday was no different. So much was going on in the world, I wanted to invest my energy in transmuting some of the hostility that was mounting on the planet. I sent a telepathic message to my gray–seal-friend in advance, hoping if he was in the bay that day, he might offer some assistance energetically.

Walking along the familiar pathway, I could feel this silent soul talk pouring out of me like liquid sunlight. My invisible message must have reached his wet nose because when I arrived, there was not only one seal to greet me, there were five! What delight. As I positioned myself on a large piece of beached driftwood to get a better look, one of the seals flopped up and out of the water in a "showing off" type of maneuver with a glee-filled telepathic announcement. "Available and ready for work ma'am." This expression left me awestruck at the wonderment of what can happen when you send out a mental message, and the recipient acknowledges with an impromptu and completely unexpected reply.

Four of the seals stayed above water; however, the fifth one submerged, possibly to facilitate the energies in a different way. I spotted a big rock on the other side of the beach to stand on for an even greater perspective and to purposefully soak in the view of my coworkers in admiration. And charmingly like dogs, the two closest to the shoreline followed me over. I would do a little dance, sing, and toss some energy their way, and they would bounce it off their slippery noses to another seal further back, and then that seal executed the same motion to another colleague at the furthest point, where the bay met the sea.

I know it sounds preposterous to say you can see energy, but I saw and sensed clairvoyantly that it was the seal's job in the last position to toss the energy out to the very deepest part of the sea for its final clearing and neutralization. They worked like a volleyball tag team rally. This all happened on the twenty-second, but since it had been given to me on a psychic level, it took until the morning of the twenty-fourth to completely understand the depth of activity.

When I had turned to head back home the morning of the incident, I didn't have the full picture. But part of me must have known because I was so full of joy and excitement I literally felt my essence exploding into millions of fragments like the light from a camera. It was simply too much for my physical body to contain, so I went off like a flash! I saw this soulful burst in my third-eye vision like a firework show of bright white lights bursting before me. The accumulated energy of a healer, enlisting help from a few ocean lightworkers, for greater peace on earth.

Truth with No Proof

Bouncing off the Walls

I prided myself on being somewhat coordinated having studied dance in my youth, so the morning I fell in the hallway going to fetch my first cup of coffee really got my attention. A few days later, I toppled over in my office as I bent down to get a cassette tape out of a storage hutch and fell and rolled over onto the floor. Almost every day that week had seen me literally bouncing off walls, and since it was so unlike me to be so physically topsy-turvy, worry was setting in.

When news came at the end of the week that the twin towers had come down on September 11, 2011, I knew I must have been tuning into the thoughts connected to the planning of this horrendous attack on the United States. It made sense from the perspective of thoughts being living things, especially when you live for a humanitarian cause with the health and well-being of planet Earth as a priority.

I had no proof it was the reason for feeling dizzy and off balance; however, perceiving the malicious threat to harm and threaten the world I am a part of was enough to knock me down. Proof enough for me.

Truth with No Proof

A Planet Named Gaia

Once upon a time, there was a planet named Earth, also known as Gaia. She'd been around for eons of time, providing a place for all of life to dwell with every possible resource needed for survival, and abundantly available, from the depth of the ocean floors to the height of ore-rich mountaintops. There was no shortage of anything on her terra firma, that is until human beings appeared on the scene.

They walked upon her surface and developed many forms of expression with the use of their free will. Some of these ways had been a detriment to the environment, and Gaia felt the calamity that ensued from mankind's choices all the way to her core. The cosmos added assistance by flooding the planet with the vibration of love for many years.

Some of this aid was delivered from space brothers and sisters, some from human beings, and some from the heavens above, which helped to permeate the dense layers of devastation surrounding earth. That is the good news. But those who were not accustomed to operating on the premise of love quickly soured and were repelled by these higher frequencies. They snapped, hit the skids you could say, by allowing their egos to overrule love and ran amuck in a modality of fear-based atrocities. As they insisted their way was the only way, they turned against themselves, each other, and everything else, leading to much violence, hatred, and loss of life.

One day having a soul chat with Gaia, I was sharing about my journey, but also choosing to hear how she was feeling about her upcoming ascension. It was her time, along with many human beings who were also choosing to ascend.[10]

I for one had incarnated to honor her evolution and the involution of my own ascension process. I loved her dearly and worried at times with all the killing and destruction if there was enough light energy for her to lift. It wasn't a topic easily broached, as most people either thought the idea was too farfetched, or that I was just off my rocker.

To compensate for that alone feeling, I'd spend as much time as possible in the reciprocal and commiserating energies of nature. I trusted my communion with the earth and soaked in

---

10. "Evolution is the developmental process of the body from the beginning of physical form until the present time. Involution is the inward process of each being's life stream energy from the inception of its essence (soul) in a body until this moment and onward. Evolution of the human form comes to completion when a person ascends; involution continues for eternity. If you are choosing to ascend, your *physical* body will continue to evolve until all cellular structures resonate to your higher God Self, ascending your physical presence into a full *light* body of soul essence." From Paula, *Inspired by Lord Buddha, One Defining Moment* (Amazon Kindle, 2015).

her wave of communication explaining to me that she felt every breath, footstep, and act of kindness generated from love. In recognition of these priceless moments, she'd let off a little snort of steam, like the way a train toot-toots and the chimney stokes as it generates enough power to get locomotion.

She was fueled with each act of love and was indeed gaining momentum. The acts of hostility and feeling taken for granted were also keenly felt by her. She gave me the image of an imaginary cylinder to demonstrate her method of coping. She would place the hostility down one side, and as each breath of love came in, she would add it to the hostility column and mix it up, so aggression would be diluted and embraced in the higher light energy—confirming that one person can make a difference.

A vision flooded me. Breath by breath, her cylinder had filled with swirling light, and a booming noise was heard, like when Cape Canaveral launches a space shuttle, only this time the rocket was earth expressing with her voice. "Lightworkers, we have lift off!" This is what will happen, the planet known as Gaia will ascend and be no more in the third dimension. She tips her hat to the new planet that will take her place and be available for those who wish to continue in human bodies and earth school ways.

Truth with No Proof

Crop of Energy

This was Gaia's time to ascend, and so the focus was upon her. Headed to Agua Dulce, I was very aware that the feeling of drudgery in my life had shifted to bliss to be of service this way. The goal was to anchor cosmic rays of energy from other planets, galaxies, and star systems, by first expanding my own light body in a ceremonial process to send out soul-ray requests.

These frequencies radiated out into the solar system to beings that had already ascended, and upon receipt of my light, they graciously exchanged with me by sending back their ascension experience in threads of unseen energy. The primary purpose of establishing a line of contact was to gain universal support for the earth, by capitalizing on the ascension technology and skills available from the outer realms. There were many times the face of a space brother or sister would pop into my mind's eye (some very unusual looking) confirming a link had been established.

It was a marvelous way to utilize experiences from the whole solar system or any other place the reality of an ascension archetype resided. As those threads of starlight would come in, my job was to collect and hold that stream of energy, waiting until Gaia herself would tell me where and when to plant it.

Then, per her request, the energy would get directed accordingly using my breath, psychic faculty, and the sheer intention to do so. My primary guide, Ascended Master Saint Germain, had made it clear that I could trust in the direction I received not only from my own body as an indicator of when energy gathered but that earth would take the next step by giving me the idea where to take these points of light.

It was an exercise in blind faith to have such confidence. My mind, of course, would have many suggestions; yet, this was not a thinking exercise, but a grand union of connecting with the soul of planet Earth. My most recent planetary lightwork had not been so happy, spending a good amount of time depressed and crying about how poorly the energies felt.

Conversely, this was a grand shift, and as I approached my destination, could feel myself radiating light drops. Just before arriving, a thought of appreciation came in for being so guided, and I formulated a directive to offer up the joy of the day's endeavor to Ashtar, a great cosmic being in league to ascend earth, and Saint Germain, my master guide.

I parked my car at the end of a deserted road and walked toward one of the dirt paths before me. Being in the high desert, there were many barren brown hills with minimal growth and an occasional cactus. I had been up some of these huge hills before and somehow knew there would be a need to come back one day, just didn't know when or why. As I started to walk up the hill, I also heard someone talking to me about the walk to Calgary and knew that more suffering was being uplifted, along with the message that Jesus had joined in. Grateful to acknowledge his presence, it brought more happiness to extend the abundance of my gifting to his essence too.

I was having fun as I walked up a very steep slope, taking little rests to lower my heart rate, and consciously pushing more energy out of my solar plexus by chanting out "Gaia!" It was my own distinct sound that resonated in those hills that day. I felt Saint Germain so close it wouldn't have surprised me to see him manifest on the spot. As I approached what I thought was the top of a steep embankment, three ravens glided by to give me a confirmation of the three masters I'd already acknowledged in prayer.

I utilized my exhale breath to extend some of this love to space and living things around me like a self-replenishing fountain gushing over the top of my head. At the top of the hill looking off in the distance, I realized there was a point higher than the one I was standing on. I said to earth, "Good thing I am in pretty good shape," not yet certain if I could go that high or needed to climb up that point. No sooner had the query presented, when a hawk flew out from the mountain crest delivering the cue to continue onward.

The crawl upward felt less strenuous once I realized the fairies and little people had joined in, not to mention leprechauns who were laughing and telling me the shoes I had on weren't the right ones to make such a climb. They had a good point because I knew some of my slipping and sliding wasn't due to bumpy terrain, but more to do with the old, worn-out horse boots I was wearing with slick flattened soles.

I took heed when the little fellows implied that a hiking boot may be in order, but also played back and forth with them, and let the little rascals know that I'd make it up the hill even with soles that had been rubbed off. I thought the play on words was funny and so did they. Souls that had been rubbed off certainly indicated the many beings that had resided and left an impression on the land beneath my feet throughout history. The air itself was getting thicker with all sorts of life forms and energy.

Reaching the cap, I watched four ravens circling, and stood quietly until Gaia showed me where to go with the first point of energy. Standing remarkably still to beckon the points of light I'd collected, breathed out a single beam pointed toward the place she'd shown me. There was a knowing the ravens were assisting in the carrying of this divine expenditure, so I put a circle around it with reverse triangles in the center to honor. With a reverent whisper, the decree was made solid. "As above, so below." *As it is in heaven, so too shall it be on earth* had sealed itself with a kiss on the land. I paused in consideration on where to go next.

The motion flowed in a similar fashion until I was aware I had directed seven points of light. That left me with two remaining. I started to walk back down and heard "twin points." Scanning the horizon, I saw what looked like twin hill tops but wasn't sure since it was a blur of one ridge folding into another. What originally looked like two became three from a different point of view back down the side of the first hill I'd climbed, so my pace quickened with anticipation of getting closer to make sure.

From a new angle, yes, it was another point with one positioned exactly at its side. A sacred vision of twin points. I knowingly directed the last two points of energy there as words that felt rehearsed for a lifetime flowed through me. The resplendent side-by-side tops bounced energy back and forth between them like the song of a comforting psalm. Just beneath their rise, a verdant slope of trees with outstretched arms for our beloved winged ones to perch had inspired my prayer.

Truth with No Proof

It was for ascension, and lay in the gentle valley between them, naked in a patch of green grass to absorb the warmth and wealth of the earth's topsoil, never to part from that embrace, the true definition of the Eternal Valley. I always felt being human was quite a challenge, but as a lightworker, my heart and soul soared. As I turned to make my way back downhill, I was feeling it was complete. Nine points of ascension light had been embedded.

Off to the side of the pathway, I was drawn to a single, orange poppy calling out to me. As I moved closer, the bright blossom offered me a message that my twin flame was there. I'd felt his energy come through me before and recognized his essence, so it had great resonance, especially because I knew he was not on this earth plane anywhere in the physical world but dwelt in the universal. So now there were four beings with me, just in case, I missed that message from the fourth raven's circling earlier on. I was thrilled to feel my twin flame after just anchoring double points of ascension energy upon those twin tops.

I thought how grand it would be to find a little memento on my way back down to the car to place on my altar as a memory of such a divine day. In a split second, my eyes covered the ground where I stood, and as I picked up a little pinkish stone, was overjoyed to find the spirit face of an owl etched upon it. There was no greater symbol of confirmation for me than that! And always given as a rest-assured sign of being at the right place at the right time.

Ignited in the cognition that earth was a living, breathing soul just like my other four loving friends came to a new revelation, "Wow that makes five!" I heard a swooshing noise and saw five ravens dancing on the swirling current of air above. An instantaneous manifestation. No lag time, and without a doubt, ascension energy.

Truth with No Proof

Ascension Flight 19

Scanning slowly for a place to sit in the large oblong room full of people waiting to board the eleven-hour flight from London to Los Angeles, I located a niche. Once seated, I noticed a man directly across from me with a distinct spiritual presence and iridescent light in his eyes that reflected much emotional sensitivity, but there was a sadness about him, and couldn't tell if it was physical, mental, or emotional. It didn't matter because I was going to facilitate anyway.

I leaned back with my head against the wall and flooded him with violet, yellow, and midnight blue light. That light then segued into a vision of the earth flooding him with her light, which graduated into an image of a golden chalice spilling pink bubbles over his head. He was being enveloped in unconditional love.

Only several minutes had passed, but when I opened my eyes he was standing, doing light yoga stretches with his back to me. It felt odd he'd positioned himself with his back to me, and even weirder he'd not given some small acknowledgment of a smile, or some little gesture to acknowledge a like-minded fellow traveler.

He was extremely stern in his manner and probably just

decided it was easier to close himself off from the rest of the world out of self-preservation. I was accustomed to sending out light anytime I saw someone who touched my heart and never felt the need to receive a thank-you. It just flows out of love; however, in this case, I sensed he was an awakened being and possibly expected more from him. At least he was up from his seat preparing his body for the long haul, which was a good sign.

Standing in line to board, the thoughts continued—if he was rejecting what I had sent by turning away, I contemplated calling back the energy to benefit myself if that was the case. It put me in a process of reminding myself not to be presumptuous about assuming everyone is open to being flooded with healing light when they may not be. Many doubts suddenly thrust themselves upon me so it was important to stick to the basics: get to my seat, put my bag and coat in the overhead, make my way to the toilet, and settle in for the journey.

Waiting outside the bathroom door, I was feeling this man close by someplace and wondered where he was seated. Moments later, the lavatory door opened, and out he came. Looking directly at me, with a soft smile on his face, in a barely audible voice said, "Thank you. Thank you very much."

Stunned, my mouth froze, so not a word fell. I could only smile and give an affirmative nod in return. Wow, people really do feel, they do sense, and they do acknowledge. Another great lesson in neutralizing judgment on people and what I think they are feeling. What mattered was the heightened level of sensitivity. Ascension energy was in motion.

It was happening. I felt confident of this as I recalled a previous communication from Ashtar when he said, "As you prepare to dwell in the 4th and 5th dimensions, the veils have become thin, and so nothing lags at this point in the spectrum. Not as much dense energy for thought forms to travel thru to find a match, or likeminded matter, which is why forms of mental telepathy between you have also quickened. You may find with regular use that you don't even need to speak as much anymore, as you see that the thought you send will be received without the need to express it verbally. As time goes on, you will find that speech itself, and the old vocabulary may not adequately convey some of your new ways and modalities of being." I smiled as I returned to my seat to sit back enjoy the remainder of the flight. Another perk manifested when the thought entered my mind that we had boarded from Gate 19 and I remembered my e-mail address.

Ascensionflight19@att.net

Truth with No Proof

Sara's Story

She had been cleaning the bathroom, Ajax in hand, when she saw a friend of hers walking down the street from their first-floor apartment window. He waved, and she acknowledged with a simple hand gesture. Her step-dad saw it and smacked her, which was embarrassing because she knew her guy friend had seen it.

Even though most of the kids in the neighborhood knew they got beat, it still was very humiliating. On some occasions, her mother would jump in with a punch or two, but not on this day, she was at work. Her four other siblings were home, but nobody dared breathe or say a word. Dearest brother, Michael, was in a wheelchair, so he was the only one exempt from the brutality.

The simple motion of waving to a friend she'd known for five years had infuriated Johnny. He further lost it when she refused to cry after the first hit, and moments later walked back over closing the bathroom door behind him and began wailing on her with clenched fists. And on it went. He was possessed in a frenzy of rage, and the only recall was trying to raise a hand to fend him off.

The measure of time seemed insignificant as to whether ten

or fifteen minutes had passed, and even though unsure about what happened next, it didn't matter, because there really didn't seem to be a choice in the matter. She was being led magnetically, and as frightened as she was, could only allow it. There were many other beings around and even though none of them looked familiar, she knew they were just ordinary people. The assessment was of being in a very different and strange place thinking, "Oh, I don't know where I am."

Then, as the pulling motion continued, a woman came forth and in a very feminine voice said, "I *am* the Mother." The pure reverence of Catholic school training left her with a startling and astonishing thought, "God is a woman!" And then, like that wasn't enough, a booming male voice filled the space, "and I *am* the Father."

The two then merged, but surprisingly she could still see both individually even though they'd become one light. Never having seen anything even remotely similar, she was in awe; however, receiving the impression that she'd have to return to earth felt very displeasing.

"Do not send me back to that toilet" was her reply. Without knowing she'd technically passed on from being knocked unconscious after hitting the toilet, the comment was uncannily accurate. The floating off into other realms brought a feeling of love and freedom not previously understood. (Sometime later it registered that it was a bath of unconditional love she'd received from Mother-Father-God.)

Now, drifting away from God's luminescent orb of light, she caught herself fighting to stay in their presence as the words spilled, "Oh, please don't go!" But fight as she might, she was told, "Return, you have much to do!" Suddenly, feeling very upset to hear her fate, mustered up all her teenage defiance in an outcry of protest, "You've got seven years!"[11]

Like a fast-forward rewind, she fell into a backward motion as she watched Mother Father getting farther and farther away. She was falling back toward earth and didn't turn around. In a moment of whirlwind energy, archangels Michael and Gabriel stood before her, and they are the ones who gave her the final push back into her tattered body with a resounding swoosh.

Literally, next to the toilet bowl was where she found herself lying when she regained consciousness, stunned and disoriented to find she was soiled from urine and defecation. She didn't have the knowledge at fourteen years old of what happens when you drop the body, and that you automatically

---

11. She was remembering her soul agreement, but based on how her life was going up to that point in time, she obviously was very upset, so giving a time ultimatum made perfect sense.

have an elimination. Not knowing how long she lay there, woke to feel flushed with humiliation, and went to lock the door so she could try to clean herself up.

Everything was a blur. It was a gross mess. She couldn't feel her face or head, but raw pain pulsed in her arms, ribs, and legs, and the thought to look in the mirror passed quickly because the focus was on getting cleaned up. Getting into the tub with her body already welting up and a vicious headache was no easy feat, and in those days with no washer or dryer, her underwear had to go into the bath. The job at hand included letting the water run out with pieces of excrement from her panties, and then a quick refill of water for cleansing purposes. No one came to the door to see if she was OK, which left her feeling even more alone and isolated.

She tried to put some soap on her face, but there was no place she could touch without intense pain. Crawling out of the tub she could barely dry herself off, and it was then that she looked at her face for the first time in the mirror. It was a look-alike for the elephant man. The swelling was so bad, she couldn't see her eyes, and black-and-blue marks were showing everywhere.

She patted her busted lip feeling the soreness of her mouth and fully understood why she found two of her teeth on the floor cleaning up. Within a couple of hours, her face was puffed out several inches. Forget about eating; she couldn't chew, and it hurt to sip.[12]

Her older sister, Rosie, was the first one to see her and could only cry at seeing how badly beaten she'd been. She reached out in a gesture of consolation, but Sara let out a yelp; no part of her could be touched because it was just too painful. Her mother came home from work but never said a word. Johnny never said a word either and left her alone for a time anyway.

As the days passed, her black-and-blue face got bigger and bigger, including split lips and slits for eyes. It was near impossible to eat with an aching jaw, and with a crack on the right side of her head bleeding, all she could do was put peroxide on it. Spirit and her guides must have done something to help, because otherwise, she *would be* dead.

What stood out in her mind was the laborious effort it took to climb the ladder every night to her bedpost on the top bunk.

---

12. Years later at a visit to the dentist, he mentioned the x-ray showed her jaw had been fractured in two places and that it didn't fuse right wondering why or if it was because she didn't go to a doctor. When she told him that she had not been to the doctor, he said, "Why not?" Sara couldn't answer his question directly, but instead replied, "I was part of the generation where child abuse was allowed." He lowered his head with a nod shaking it in sorrow, and they went on. At fifty-something years old, she let him know she wasn't choosing to have it rebroken to heal properly.

She was barely able to move, and it took forever; once she managed to get up there, she could only sleep on her back. So there was no relief during the day and no rest at night. In modern day, arrests would have been made, and the children would have been removed from the home.

Seven Years Later

At age twenty-one, seven years later to the date of her first meeting with Mother-Father-God, awoke on the living-room floor with her seven-year-old nephew shaking her by the shoulder and asking her if she was dead. She'd fainted. Her family were in a panic and scrambled for her friend Josie a couple of doors down who managed to lift her up on the bed and call 911. They took her by ambulance to a nearby medical center only to be received by an unsympathetic doctor asking, "What is she on?"

On a gurney in the hospital hallway unable to speak due to massive pain shooting up the side of her neck, she didn't know what to expect. But he insisted, "What is she on?" Assuming it was drugs, he determined they couldn't take care of her there and had her wheeled back into the ambulance. Sirens blaring, she passed out again.

This time when she opened her eyes, there seemed to be a little more compassion in play when the EMT patted her and said, "Don't worry, haven't lost anyone yet." Not wanting to startle her already-terrified mother in the front seat, she took off the oxygen mask, but the courtesy was not acceptable to the ambulance tech who promptly repositioned the mask on her face. Weird how things work out. The next stop was the same hospital she'd been to a week prior telling medical staff she was nauseous and feeling pregnant, but they insisted she was not. Ambulance doors swinging open, she ripped off the oxygen mask one more time not to upset her mother (which was a different sort of ache). As they wheeled her in the hallway, she yelled out, "Help me!" in ridiculous pain.

A nurse got her in a room, but after taking her blood pressure dropped the device and ran out stopping the first doctor she saw. After a few words to him, he threw his files on the floor, and they both came running back into the room. The doctor must have asked for another reading on her blood pressure because she remembered the nurse saying, "Her pressure is dropping, I can't hold it."

Sara went unconscious and found herself in the same unusual place she'd been seven years earlier with people passing back and forth, but not because she was on forty-second street. It was a similar feeling of excitement and being pulled. Then, exactly, the same situation as before. "I *am* the Mother," the delicate voice said, with Father appearing seconds later. She remembered the joy to feel that kind of love again and knew she was in the presence of God.

Her consciousness had been expanded from the previous

encounter, so she could properly address them now as Mother-Father-God. The sight was of Mother and Father again as one but also retaining the familiar distinction of two. The overall sense was that things had changed, and she was on a new pathway with much to do.

The imagery was the same as the first death experience, only this time a being came into her line of vision wearing a Maltese Cross pendant, and it was all she could see in that moment because it was literally glistening. He was bathed in purple light and was glowing, and as he came toward her, she could see he was in a purple robe. Standing before her extending his hands, palms up, she instinctively knew to lay her hands atop of his, palms down.

There was no resistance as his energy filled her from head to toe, and she yielded to the notion of having to come back to earthly life one more time. Then he stepped to the side, and as she turned to face Mother-Father-God, it was to thank them for loving her so much. With that communication given, the purple man took her by the hand, and that is how she recalled reentering her body in death experience round two.

Regaining consciousness, and aware enough to know she was fully back in her body, found her legs splayed open and the doctor talking over her with a set of cardiac paddles that weren't in the room before. He said, "Is there anyone with you?" She couldn't talk but nodded her mother was there. He continued, "You have a tubal pregnancy that has ruptured, you have lost a lot of blood and will need immediate surgery or you will die." (Little did he know she already had.)

Her husband got there quickly after being notified by her mother, and after monitoring the situation, didn't want the intern on duty in the operating room, and instead, insisted on the head of the hospital. After much fuss, it was the chief of staff who performed the surgery that saved her life.

A memory flashed of the anesthetist telling her people have said the medicine tastes like garlic, and after having that taste burst in her mouth replied, "They are right." Everything went black. She was greeted by the purple man's face, and yet, the majesty of his entirety was like being in the presence of the almighty everything.

"The love, there is no way to define it or put it in a box, or a circle, it is just surrounding you and going through you," she described. The incredible feeling of love is what she remembered coming back to life, and after receiving five bags of blood during surgery, also distinctly recalled there was no resistance in returning to her body like the first time she visited the spirit realm.

She became a channel for the purple man, Ascended Master Saint Germain, confirming her mission on earth was not yet complete. Although she could have exercised her free will at any time, I, for one, am so grateful she stayed.

Truth with No Proof

Bibliography

Bourassa, Paula. *Inspired by Lord Buddha, One Defining Moment.* Amazon Kindle, 2015.

Bourassa, Paula, and Ascended Master Kuthumi. *Love Is Enough.* LuLu.com, 2012.

www.ingramcontent.com/pod-product-compliance
Lightning Source LLC
Chambersburg PA
CBHW061323040426
42444CB00011B/2752